The Descent into Happiness

A Bicycling Journey
over the Cascades and Rockies and
across the Great Plains

D0710117

David Howell

BLUE EAR BOOKS

Published in 2016 by
Blue Ear Books
7511 Greenwood Ave N, Box 400
Seattle, WA 98103
USA

www.blueearbooks.com

ISBN: 978-0-9844063-6-4

Credits:

Cover Art:
  Kaitlyn Howell
Cover Design:
  Balzac Communications, Napa, CA
Book Composition:
  Jennifer Haywood, Blue Ear Books, Seattle, WA
Printer:
  Scott Morris, Morris Printing Services, Arkansas City, KS, www.morrisprint.com

For Sue

CONTENTS

We must have the stubbornness to accept our gladness
in the ruthless furnace of this world.

— Jack Gilbert, *Refusing Heaven*

PROLOGUE

In the summer of 2015 I rode my bicycle from Seattle to Milwaukee. I wanted to make the ride because I had read the blogged stories of others who had taken on the Northern Tier, a route that goes over the North Cascades Highway, through Glacier National Park, and along Highway 2 across the Great Plains, all the way back to my home in Wisconsin.

It was a great experience. Bicycling is, among other things, a thought process. The more slowly you ride a bike, and the longer you ride a bike, the more slowly you think, the longer you engage in a certain depth of thought.

The reverse is also true. The faster you ride your bike, the quicker your thoughts become. Mountain biking is a good example of this: If you don't react quickly—if you don't think in terms of immediate reaction—you're likely to ride your bike into a tree or through a bush. You have to pay attention; you have to think quickly from moment to moment, until the ride becomes one ongoing moment. You have to be mentally present.

Bike touring is the other end of the spectrum. You spend day after day out on the road, just rolling along, lost in thought. At least, that's true if you bike alone. In the company of others bicycling becomes a communal activity, a vehicle for conversation. When my kids were growing up, we would go on long bike rides and bike camping adventures. At first the kids were in a bike trailer; then they graduated to the trail-a-bike, then to the back of a tandem, and eventually to their own bikes. Each successive bike-related vehicle changed the type of conversation we had. What amazed me was how candid my children were in our discussions; they would say anything. Even into their teenage years, bicycling seemed to be that time when we engaged in authentic conversation. It's how I found out about my daughter's relationships, about my son's love of theatre.

Solo bike touring is, for me, a vehicle for thought, for dialogue with one's self. I'm a big fan of talking to myself, of thinking in complete sentences. And there's no better place to do that than on an open road. The more road, the better.

When I'm at work—as a professor in a Humanities Department at a school of engineering—I think in small chunks. At work, there are too many things to do in a given day: grade papers, teach classes, conduct office hours, respond to emails. In the worst-case scenario, I overlap these tasks. The tasks do connect and weave together, but the thought process required is one that moves from one place to another at a quick pace: more mountain biking than touring, more reaction than reflection.

Which is why I went on a big bike tour from Seattle, where I was born and grew up, to Milwaukee, where I currently live. I wanted my mind to slow down as much as possible, just as I wanted the bike to roll along slowly. I wanted to engage in thought for a sustained period of time, so I could experience thoughts to their completion. No interruptions. No dialogue.

"Journeys are the midwives of thought," writes Alain de Botton. "Few places are more conducive to internal conversations than moving planes, ships or trains. There is an almost quaint correlation between what is before our eyes and the thoughts we are able to have in our heads: large thoughts at times requiring large views, and new thoughts, new places. Introspective reflections that might otherwise be liable to stall are helped along by the flow of the landscape."

Imagine riding your bike over the North Cascades Highway, over the Going-to-the-Sun Road in Glacier National Park, across North Dakota. It's that landscape that I wanted my body and mind to engage in, if for no other reason than to find out what thoughts, quite literally, came to mind.

WASHINGTON

DAY ONE

It's good to start a journey surrounded by friends and family, especially if you intend to travel alone. This morning I started this adventure at the home of my friends Denny and Suzanne, where they let my family and me stay for a couple of days. The trip will take five to six weeks to complete, which made it difficult to leave this happy little group of people who in large part define who I am. Leaving my wife Sue was especially difficult. I haven't been away from her for more than two weeks at a time since we were married twenty-five years ago; now I'm going to be gone for well over a month.

I've been planning this ride for a year, ever since Sue gave me a touring bike for my 50th birthday. She drove me to our local bike shop, walked me to the center of the store, and said, "Choose which one you want." I knew the one I wanted; I'd been eyeing it for months. I chose a 2014 Salsa Vaya, a sport-touring bike designed to carry fifty pounds of cargo for days on end. The potential this bike had to offer was long-term; many adventures were possible, now that the bike was going to be part of my life.

I like naming my bikes. Countless hours are spent riding them, working on them, dreaming of the places that bikes can go. This bike I simply named Salsa.

But the gift was more than the bike. It was Sue's willingness to let me pursue an experience that would require a stretch of time. This trip has actually been in the back of my head for quite a while. I've traversed the country on planes, in cars, and on motorcycles, but never on a bicycle. A bike requires more time and contact with one's surroundings. And going on my own affords me the chance not only to ride the bike, but also to reflect on a series of ideas I've been contemplating for a decade. One such idea is how much I love my wife, how much I love to be alone, and how those two things are sometimes at odds with each other. It's a good problem to have, to love someone else's company as well as your own. Maybe when this trip ends I'll understand better how the two connect.

I left Denny and Suzanne's 25 miles ago. Now I'm sitting on a picnic table on the edge of Puget Sound, looking west at the Olympic Mountains, all trees and snow-crested peaks. I'm looking forward to the hours of biking each day of this ride, but I'm also anticipating moments like this, when I get off the bike and look around.

Because I'm a professor who teaches on a nine-month contract, summers represent a break from work. For the last twenty years, summers have focused on spending time with the kids. But now my daughter Kait is in college and working at an outdoor adventure camp, and my son Evan is turning seventeen and has established his domestic independence. I no longer have to take care of them. Now I can take care of myself with a gift of solitude, the stretch of time that lies before me.

It was auspicious that the trip began with Denny and Suzanne, two of the most amply generous people I will ever meet. Denny is a fellow cyclist. I had my bike shipped to his house, and it was damaged in transit: a broken spoke and bent derailleur hanger, repairs I can't attempt myself with certainty. So Denny called a friend who runs the local bike shop and, even though it was the Fourth of July and the shop was closed, his friend opened his shop to perform the emergency repair. An hour later, the bike was fixed and ready to roll. I've read on bicycling blogs that I'd meet good people by going on a long bike ride, that riding across the country helps restore your faith in humanity. I just didn't think it would happen before the trip even began.

I need to meet more good people. I don't have many friends. As an introvert, I have trouble meeting people. Actually, I don't have trouble meeting people, because I don't often make the attempt. I have ample contact with students and colleagues at the university, and I enjoy spending as much time as possible with the wife and kids. It's just that solitude, time alone in the office or at home before the fireplace, provides inward rejuvenation. Hours spent alone don't leave much time for interacting with others. Hopefully, this ride will enable that to happen.

It's the end of the first day, and my hope has already come true: I met good people. I contacted a host via Warm Showers, an online community that enables bike tourists to stay at the homes of people who are willing to allow cyclists to pitch their tents in their yards. Sometimes they even provide a good meal. This is what happened this evening; I contacted Bill and Ann Testerman in Anacortes, Washington, and they invited me to stay with them. Not only did they let me put my tent in their yard, but they also let me take a shower and invited me to share dinner. I'm sure there will be difficult days on this journey; it's good that today, the first day, is not one of them.

One of the classes I teach focuses on Servant-Leadership. In that class we talk a great deal about leadership theory. One of the tenets of the Servant-Leadership model is empathy, the ability to understand and share the feelings of another. At the onset of this trip, I met three people who empathized with me: one who fixed my bike because he knew my journey wouldn't happen without the repair and a couple who love to bike tour and enjoy sharing their home with other travelers. It makes me wonder if today is a fluke, or if this breadth of generosity will continue for the next five weeks. Maybe the trick to meeting good people is simply to put yourself out there: to have a need and express it, so someone can help meet it.

DAY TWO

This morning I got lost three times, each time in a town I had to ride through to get into the mountains. Twice I asked for help, and the people I approached were more than willing to point me in the right direction.

I thought about this today on the bike: the idea, or metaphor if you will, that I got lost only in towns. After making it through Burlington and Sedro Woolly, I stayed on roads running parallel to Highway 20, a freeway bordered by mountains to the north and the Skagit River to the south. It's literally impossible to get lost on such roads, which is something worth contemplating. I used to live in rural environments: a cabin outside Fairbanks, Alaska and a double-wide trailer north of Pullman, Washington. In those places there was no geographic unknown; particular mountains were always on the horizon. When I moved to Milwaukee, it took several years to figure out where I was at any given moment. I still occasionally get lost, which is not altogether a bad thing as you get to know a city. But when you travel through a place like the landscape I'm biking through, it's just one extra thing you don't have to worry about.

Everyone seems to be flocking to cities. I've read the statistics on how many of my students will live in urban environments. If they do well in their careers, they might be able to afford a cabin "up north," a place to go on weekends to escape from the physical and mental congestion of the city. Most of my students hail from small towns in Wisconsin; they choose to attend my university in part because it's located in the heart of downtown Milwaukee. It makes me wonder if they'll ever return to rural life, and whether Sue and I will ever leave the urban.

There must be a connection between the quality of the people I'm meeting on this trip and the landscape they live in. It's something I need to research: empathy and landscape.

At the end of today's ride I was happy to get to the campground at Ross Lake, because I had biked for 90 miles. I was so happy, after months of planning, finally to be on the bike that I couldn't help myself; I just kept going for twelve hours straight. Regardless, the campsite was a welcome sight, because I wanted to continue in the solitude I enjoyed all day on the bike. But it wasn't to be, because Paco, who was in the next campsite, offered me a beer. One of my rules in life is, "Never say no to a beer." When someone offers you a beer, they usually also offer you their story, and that's exactly what happened with Paco. He told me about the village he comes from in Spain, how he loves to travel and will take years off from his career to see the world. We discussed the merits and drawbacks of jobs in high tech: how you have to stay on top of your game if you hope to stay gainfully employed, and how difficult that is when you want to walk away from the job for years at a time. Still, he makes this conscious choice, to travel to places like north-central Washington, surrounded by mountains that he will be hiking through for the remainder of the week before flying to Chile to do more of the same.

I had to remind myself to be present during our conversation, to enjoy his story, because what I really wanted was to be alone. Thank goodness for rules and beer.

Tomorrow I will ride over a mountain pass, the first of five. I hope biking 90 miles today left enough energy for a 5000-foot climb up Rainy Pass and Washington Pass.

DAY THREE

It was a good day, climbing 5,400 feet through North Cascades National Park. The views were breathtaking: snowcapped peaks in the heat of July, vertical rock formations in every direction. I spent about half of the day in my smallest gear, traveling at 4.7 miles per hour. It's a slow pace, but one of this trip's purposes is to go as slowly as possible.

Temperatures have been hitting the high nineties mid-day, so I've been waking up at four in the morning and on my bike by five. I consider myself a morning person, but waking at four is a stretch. It's cool in the morning, and I'm enjoying the sunrise. Today was especially engaging because the sun would rise above a mountain and, as I biked the mountain pass, it would go away, only to re-appear along another ridge, then hide again behind an even taller mountain.

The morning provided complete silence. Mountain silence. No cars or semi trucks on the road for the first three hours of today's ride.

Starting early also means the ride is done by noon, providing the opportunity to do other things than ride the bike. Like sit and think.

Going slow is difficult when you're not accustomed to it. Like many things on this trip, it's a learned skill. I try to slow down my day-to-day life, but it's difficult. I've chosen a career in teaching so I can spend ample hours each day in a tranquil university office, but that doesn't mean things slow down. Technology gets in the way: the bombardment of email, grading student essays on the university online learning management tool, teaching hybrid courses. It's never-ending. Fortunately, this trip became possible. I find myself, though, here in rural Washington State, seeking out wi-fi networks so I can email friends and family. I want to be alone out here, but I still use available tech to keep in touch with loved ones.

Before I was a university professor I spent eight years in high tech, working for Microsoft and Microsoft Partners. There is nothing slow about modern technology and, even though I enjoyed working with smart people, the pace of the work was damaging. I hope that by the end of this trip I will have learned how to be slow, then to implement that learned skill into my daily work and personal life.

I'm out here riding my bike in part because I hope to meet people who know how to go slow. It gets back to the idea of empathy, because empaths are good listeners, and active listening requires one to pay attention to what the other person is saying. That takes time and intentionality. I'm finding it happening already.

Tonight, I'm staying at a bicycles-only campsite between Mazama and Winthrop. I was hoping to have the site to myself, but three young men who just graduated from college arrived, and we ended up having a great conversation about their bike ride from Washington D.C. They have only three days left on their journey, and I'm only three days into mine. I asked them all kinds of questions: where it's most difficult or dangerous to ride, what they do for food, how many miles they go in a day, how they determine their routes. They were a wellspring of information. Then a couple from Copenhagen arrived, and soon six of us were engaged in discussion, so I excused myself and went to my tent.

While riding today, I thought a great deal about ignorance. I embrace the dictionary definition of ignorance: simply not knowing about a given subject or topic. Though I've been riding a bicycle my whole life, and though I've seen much of the world, I feel very ignorant when it comes to bicycle touring. It's a new and all-consuming subject. These three young men know all about it, because they've been living it for the last 49 days. I asked if they're ready for it to end. After some thought they said yes, it's time for the next big thing—they just don't know what the next thing is.

DAY FOUR

I awoke again at four a.m. so I could beat the afternoon heat, a good decision given that the first half of today's ride was over Loup Loup Pass, an assent of 4,020 feet. I'm learning to ride slowly, pedaling exclusively in the granny gear and taking pleasure in it. I've ridden my motorcycle over Loup Loup Pass many times, but I never took a good look at it before because I was always focused on the road. Going four and a half miles per hour through a turn is very different than blasting through the same turn at eighty.

Because of the slow pace, I was able to see detail. A fire devastated the area a year ago. I studied the stark, burnt trees in the valleys, timbers cut near the edge of the road to prevent the fire from jumping. In the mountains of northern Washington, you grow accustomed to riding through lush green landscapes; that's what made this charred topography so striking. The morning air was cool, but it was overwhelmed by the smell of charcoal, the scent of the countless blackened timbers, overwhelmed.

At the start of the climb was a box by the roadside full of water bottles, with a notebook filled with comments from previous cyclists. On the side of the box was a drawing of a bicycle in crayon, with the words "Cold Water. Take one."

I have five weeks to learn how to slow down. The other cyclists I've met so far, the ones who have been on the road for months or years, have an ease to them that I find uncommon. They have only a few things to concern themselves with: what to eat, where to sleep, which direction to go.

On the first day of the trip, I was anxious because I kept getting lost on the map. The maps I'm using, produced by the Adventure Cycling Association (ACA), provide ample detail regarding the recommended route for a bicyclist, distances between locations, directions on where to turn to navigate through townships, road gradation, campsites, grocery stores, libraries, hotels. But all that data was consuming my attention; I was focusing so hard on the map that I was going off route. There were stretches of time those first couple of days when I was not paying attention to the panorama around me, so focused was I on what it looked like on the map.

The three college grads had been using the same set of maps. When I told them my frustration with focusing on the map to the exclusion of everything else, they laughed and said they had done the same thing. Their solution was to decide that only one of them would be responsible for the map, and that instead of placing it in the map holder on top of the tank bag, the "map man" would put it in the back pocket of his bike shorts. If he needed to consult it he would take it out, then put it back again. Problem solved.

Today, I paid less attention to the map. As the opportunities to take wrong turns dissipate as the maps take me deeper into the mountains, so does the concern about getting lost. It will be a moot issue by the time I reach eastern Montana and North Dakota, where the route is one long straight line of old highway.

Graham, one of the three college graduates, received his degree in philosophy. His thesis focused on Buddhism and 20th-century feminist studies. I asked him if everyone was concerned for his future gainful employment, and he said yes—but he's not. He knows he received a good education. He knows that opportunity lies before him. I asked what he was going to do next, and he said he plans to hike the Appalachian Trail—again—this time south to north. After that he isn't sure what he'll do, but he knows it will be an extension of the bike ride, the hike, and his degree. That's all the map he needs.

It's noon now, and I'm resting beneath a shade tree in a park in Riverside, Washington. I've already put seven hours on the bike and have traveled 64 miles, most of them going over Loup Loup. There's no hurry to get to where I'm staying tonight; it's only fifteen miles down the road. The temperature is in the high nineties. No need to hurry.

It turned out to be in the hundreds. One hundred and seven degrees, to be exact. The final fifteen miles were brutal. Between mountain passes, the scenery shifted to flat and brown, and there was no wind to push or pull me along. Double-wide trailers at the end of dirt driveways seemed to fit the landscape. There were some horses ambling around the trailers, looking for something green to eat. All I could do was try not to think about how hot it was and how far I had to go.

It's nice to have a dry heat, as opposed to the humidity of the Midwest. But still. Once I arrived at the Visitor Center in Tonasket, a community resource that provides free bicycle camping in the lawn behind their building, I got out the laptop and map and adjusted the plan. I was hoping to climb two mountain ranges tomorrow, but the forecast is for an even hotter day. I contacted a Warm Showers host in Republic, a mining town 40 miles from here, and she eagerly agreed to host me. Once again, I'm confronted by the generosity of strangers. That makes tomorrow a lighter day: one mountain pass, 40 miles, all done in the morning. The day after that will be longer, but cooler. I've come to realize that the air in the mountains in Washington is different, somehow unadulterated. I can actually feel the change in the air, the fresh oxygen I breathe.

I have this space to myself. I have to admit that in spite of my desire to be alone, a part of me hopes some group of cyclists will come rolling up with their stories. This is the fourth day of my journey, and it's the first evening I'm by myself, here at the Visitor Center.

But in truth, I'm not really alone. I called Sue to ask how her day went, and I also talked with her at length this morning. I phoned my mom because today is her birthday. Then I sent an email with photos of the day to other friends and family, something I've done every day of the trip so far. So although I talk about being alone, really I'm just by myself, which is not the same.

But I do have an entire day to be, physically, by myself. The first thing I did when I arrived was to head to the gas station down the street and buy a can of beer, which I then enjoyed at the Visitor Center, sitting in the shade of a building, watching two birds call to each other for a good hour.

DAY FIVE

It turned out I wasn't alone last night. Just as I was preparing dinner, twin brothers from Omaha whom I had met earlier in my ride came rolling into the campsite. I offered to share my meal, quinoa with sautéed onions and yellow squash purchased at a roadside stand the day before. But they opted instead to eat what they eat every night: five peanut butter and jelly sandwiches, each. It was amazing to watch them consume all that food. When I had first met the twins several days earlier in front of a grocery store in Concrete, they were splitting a large box of Trix cereal. The three college students told me they go through a large jar of peanut butter every day, on top of a regimented diet of rice and beans. I'm not consuming food in mass quantities. Not yet.

For long-distance events one needs a good nutritional strategy, but one of the reasons I want to do this ride is to drop some weight. Several years ago, when I changed my career from professor to Dean of Students, I used food to cope with the added professional stress. Although I gave up that job for a long list of reasons, what I didn't give up was the weight. I entered this ride a good thirty pounds heavy.

It's a conundrum, because I love to exercise and I love to eat. Before this trip I took part in triathlons, competing in six Ironman distance events. I would lose weight during the training season, only to put it back on afterward. This bike ride should provide ample time to reflect on why I want to drop weight, because I know it's more a mental issue than a physical one.

What do I love to eat? All the carb-heavy concoctions of a typical Midwestern diet: chocolate cake, cream pies, extra-cheesy mac-n-cheese. But what I want to do with my life is to think well and exercise well, and I want to shift from a wheat-based diet to one packed with proteins and fats. It may be that, on this ride, away from the habitual delicacies available in Milwaukee, I'll be able to change the way I consume food. Being lighter would enable me to do better what I enjoy most: thinking while riding my bike.

To understand why being light on the bike enhances performance, one need only turn to Newton's second law of motion: $F = MA$. Less mass means less acceleration needed to create the necessary force.

To understand why eating fewer carbs provides better mental performance requires a different type of scientific understanding. I've been reading countless articles lately about how the body needs to consume fat for best cognitive performance. Fewer carbs, more fats. I love to think, so if eating food that's good for the brain will help me do that, so be it.

The desire to eat better on the ride didn't stop me from consuming a plate full of pancakes when I arrived in Republic. I headed straight to the diner with the intent of having a Cobb salad, but instead devoured one of my all-time favorite meals. God, I love pancakes.

I also want to drop weight so I can in order to look better for Sue. She eats better than I do, and it shows. My son asked me recently what my "type" of woman was, and I immediately told him: about 5' 10", athletic build, brown eyes, long brunette hair. He rolled his eyes, because I had just described his mother (sans the long hair). I know it's not for my benefit that she stays trim, but I must admit that it's nice having a smokin' hot wife. I should return the favor.

In the spirit of eating well on this trip, I did decide to bring my Optimus 99 camp stove in order to prepare meals along the way. I've been using this stove for more than thirty years. It means carrying additional weight: the stove itself, plus a canister of white gas and cooking gear. But it provides culinary options. The bicycle blogs I read to prepare for this trip were filled with people looking for prepared food the entire route. In some parts of the country, including the small towns I'll be going through in eastern Montana and North Dakota, the only place you can find easy food is in local taverns. As much as I love tavern food, I hope to stick to grocery stores in pursuit of fresh produce and protein. To eat well is to think well and to bike well.

Today I climbed Wauconda Pass, elevation 4,310 feet. While biking up the pass, I imagined a new diet: the Northern Tier Weight Loss Program. You too can drop 30 pounds in 30 days by following three simple steps:

- Step 1: acquire a fully loaded touring bike
- Step 2: ride it for 8 hours
- Step 3: repeat Step 2 thirty times

We'll see where I'm at when this trip ends.

It's time to refuel, which means avoiding a meal at the Republic Pizza Company, as good as that sounds, and instead eat healthy.

I have another Warm Shower stay, the family of Patty and Ron Slagle. Ron graciously offered me some salmon to grill up, fish he caught last summer off Kodiak Island.

DAY SIX

Not only did Patty and Ron provide a salmon dinner, they also prepared a portable breakfast of two egg-and-bacon bagels, a brownie, and a Tupperware container of fresh raspberries. Before yesterday they had never met me, yet they shared their home, time, and company with me.

I ate one of those bagels before starting the day's ride at 5:00 a.m. So far on this trip I haven't been doing that, opting instead to bike for an hour and then pull over for a morning snack. Beginning the day with calories ready to burn made a big difference.

And burn they did. Leaving Republic I summited Sherman Pass, elevation 5,575 feet. Climbing mountain passes early in the morning has been ideal. The logging trucks are not yet on the road, so I have the entire landscape to myself. I love to climb. It's hard work, pulling the bike up the mountainside in the lowest gear. After three hours of ascending Sherman Pass, I descended with a maximum speed of 37.5 miles per hour as I flew down a 22-mile drop into Kettle Falls, a town saddled beside the Columbia River.

On the way down I had a flat. The logging trucks leave small shards of metal that fly off their tires and wreak havoc on bicycle tires. Fixing it was easy, but my frustration came in having another flat later in the day. It was a slow leak, so I pumped air into the tire periodically to keep it going, until I reached a campground in the mountains above Iona late in the day. There I was able to examine the tire closely, only to realize that the rear tire was already showing signs of wear, and I'm only six days into the trip. I opted to switch the front and rear tires, to provide more tread on the back of the bike. I'll have to keep an eye on that tire. The last real bike shop is in Whitefish, Montana. After that, any solutions to bicycle maintenance issues will have to be somewhat creative.

I was surprised at how happy I felt to summit Sherman Pass. It wasn't from the sense of accomplishment, climbing four mountain passes in six days. It was more a sense of earned work. My favorite philosopher, Nishida Kitaro, founder of the Kyoto School of philosophy, distinguishes pleasure from happiness. We suffer for what makes us happy, he says. Pleasure does not involve suffering. The things that truly give me happiness—my wife and children, my career, this bike ride—involve sacrifice and work. My legs were hurting, but they were happy.

It was good to reflect on Nishida's sense of happiness as I watched the sun climb in the sky, before descending the mountain.

IDAHO

DAY SEVEN

Today is a rest day. One day in Idaho. It only takes about eight hours to bike across the northern part of Idaho's panhandle.

I crossed the Washington-Idaho border yesterday afternoon and biked to Denny and Suzanne's cabin on Spirit Lake, a 1920s-era hunting lodge in its original condition. A few amenities have been added over the years, such as a coffee maker and toaster, but that's about it.

My legs are ready to rest. It was hard to climb out of bed this morning, and it took a good ten minutes for my quads and hamstrings to limber up. Some stretching should become part of my daily regimen. My mind is also ready to rest.

Before arriving at the cabin, I stopped in the township of Spirit Lake to tap into the complementary wi-fi at the local coffee shop. Then, it was off to the grocery store to purchase a six-pack of Deschutes Black Butte Porter, a T-bone steak (which somehow cost only $8.50), some broccoli, an apple, an orange, butter, and a dozen eggs. At the cabin I made phone calls to my parents, my son, my daughter, my wife, Denny and Suzanne. It was good to talk to them all and let them know I had arrived at the cabin and am taking a day off. It was also good to get the correspondence out of the way so I could shut down my brain and focus only on how best to season the T-bone.

The first week of the bike ride has been exhilarating. I'm grateful for everything I've learned so far. But the data intake has been overwhelming: studying the map to make sure I'm on track, determining the distance to the next water and food stop, checking the bike computer for rate of speed, checking the mirror for traffic from behind, taking in the view. It's exhilarating, but exhausting.

In another week, I'll better understand the process of bicycle touring. More subject-matter expertise. More awareness of known variables. Knowing how the bike performs, how long it takes to get from one point to another, the patterns of conversation among bike tourists. It will become easier, not only because the body adapts to the rigor of riding eighty miles a day, but because the mind does as well.

In the West we tend to separate the body from the mind, physiology from psychology. One reason I've been a student of Eastern philosophy over the years is the lack of "ologies." Eastern philosophy, generally speaking, connects and blends disciplines. My doctoral dissertation was interdisciplinary for this very reason: I was more interested in connecting various academic subjects than in becoming a specialist in one. I enjoy talking to people with a similar passion for deep yet general knowledge. It's in large part what interests me in my wife's study of veterinary medicine. She has to be a specialist not only in dogs and cats, but also in pigs, birds, goats, whatever comes through the door of her clinic. What she learns from one patient informs her treatment of the next, and as the years go by she becomes a subject-matter expert not just on one problem regarding one species, but on a myriad of issues spread across a variety of patients of various species.

I enjoy learning about bike touring in part because I already know a great deal about road biking, mountain biking, bicycle commuting, triathlon, Ironman training. If it has something to do with cycling it piques my interest, especially if it cross-pollinates from one cycling subsection to another. I know how to descend a mountain safely on a fully loaded touring bike because my friend Rich, who is a seasoned mountain biker, taught me that you turn the bicycle not with the handlebar but by transferring pressure to the saddle from the inside of your thigh. In doing so, you turn the bike from the center of your own body as well as the center of the bike, thus making for a controlled turn at 35 miles per hour. Similarly, I learned how to descend mountain passes quickly by training for Ironman. You have to learn to go fast, because the point of that sport is to go fast for a long time. It's my hope that I'm quickly adapting to bike touring because I've spent the last 40 years on a variety of bicycles for different purposes. If I keep learning how to ride a different kind of bike, then biking will continue to provide a wellspring of happiness.

Nishida Kitaro's *An Inquiry into the Good* is one of my all-time favorite books. I think so highly of it that I make it a required text in my university Ethics classes. Its title initially caught my interest because I want to be good at what I do, regardless of what I'm doing. But I was not prepared for what I read in Nishida's seminal work.

For starters I wasn't well read in Eastern philosophy at the time, which made Nishida's concepts difficult to comprehend. That required doing some background reading on both Eastern and Western philosophy, since Nishida actually built a philosophical bridge between Zen Buddhism and Kantian metaphysics.

After years of reading Nishida, I decided to pursue a Ph.D. and to use his concept of "the good" as the theoretical cornerstone of a doctoral thesis. It meant that much to me to understand how to be good at something. It's still a cornerstone of my metaphysic, my way of interpreting reality, because goodness, or happiness—I equate the two—is not something we stumble upon. People are not happy because they fall into it. Rather, people who possess deep-seated happiness find it because they have a method. It was because my method to find happiness involves embracing hard work, and because climbing Sherman Pass was hard work, that after summiting it I felt deeply happy. You could say that that, for me, happiness is something to experience, rather than something to acquire.

Nishida's take on "experience" is not about the pursuit of happiness. Rather, for Nishida happiness is a result of "pure experiencing." Here is how he defines it:

> To experience means to know facts just as they are, to know in accordance with facts by completely relinquishing one's own fabrications. What we usually refer to as experience is adulterated with some sort of thought, so by pure I am referring to the state of experience just as it is without the least addition of deliberative discrimination.

I was happy climbing and summiting the pass because I wasn't thinking about what I was doing; I was just doing it. I enjoyed the first couple of days of this trip, but I had to think a great deal about what I was doing. Whereas by the time I reached Sherman Pass, I had processed enough knowledge that I didn't have to give it deliberation.

Nishida goes on to say that, in true Buddhist tradition, experience is best when there is no separation between subject and object:

> When one directly experiences one's own state of consciousness, there is not yet a subject or an object, and knowing and its object are completely unified. This is the most refined type of experience.... A truly pure experience has no meaning whatsoever; it is simply a present consciousness of facts just as they are.

The work my body was involved in as I climbed Sherman Pass, the mountain air I inhaled, the feel of sunlight cresting the ridge, the sound of ravens cawing: such an experience requires not having thoughts such as *How much longer is this going to take?* or *I need to take a fucking break!* You don't control the thought. Instead, you allow thought simply to become part of the experience. When that happens, I'm intensely happy.

That's why I enjoyed Sherman Pass the most. It was the fourth pass summited in four days, so I didn't have to learn as much. The variables were known, so the mind could engage in what the body was doing.

This can be applied to any area of subject-matter expertise, though it helps if the area of interest is somewhat complex. You know your subject area, you experience your subject area, and that experience has the potential to make you happy. There is struggle in learning, especially if what you're trying to do is difficult. My son loves to play the cello because he will spend his entire life learning how to play it. My daughter is studying Mandarin because she embraces the complexity and nuances of Chinese language and culture. I love my wife because she is a complicated woman who grows and changes every day of her life. And I love bicycling, but I have to experience it in new and different ways, in order to keep the learning fresh and sustain this sense of deep-seated happiness. The more I do this, the more I become expert at experiencing the bike, the more I tap into that sense of "pure".

"Slow," from my experience, is critical. As experience purifies it slows down. Nishida was a master of zazen, the Japanese discipline of "just sitting." What's the slowest activity you can think of? Sitting, breathing, staring at a blank wall. I am not an expert at zazen; I lack the patience for it. I appreciate Nishida's concept of pure experience because it takes the concept of "just sitting" and transfers it to any and all activity. It's like meditation in motion.

Sports psychologists use the term "flow" to describe this. In *Creativity: Flow and the Psychology of Discovery and Invention*, Mihaly Csikszentmihalyi writes about how athletes lose themselves to sport if they have certain prerequisites: you have to be in good physical condition, possess expert knowledge on the sport, and be "one" with those you play with.

Flow is slow—even if what you are doing happens at high rates of speed.

What I want to learn from this big bike ride I'm on is how to sustain that sense of flow for as long as possible. That's why I want to ride the bike slowly for eight hours at a time and for weeks on end: it's the process of "becoming one" with the bike, the act of the subject (me) embracing the object (the bike) to the point where we're one machine rolling down the road.

It's as if the first-person pronoun, the "I", is removed. No longer is it "I ride my bike"; rather, it's just "bicycling." It's not "my legs hurt" but just "legs hurt."

There's also happiness in knowing that a great deal of forethought and preparation went into making this happen. Finding happiness on Sherman Pass was no accident.

But enough of these musings. Today is a rest day, so I should take a break from thinking about cycling.

One last thought. If Nishida distinguishes pleasure from happiness by saying that we suffer for what makes us happy, then descending the mountain pass gave pleasure. Climbing it allowed for happiness.

I began this narrative using words such as "journey" and "adventure." That was before the journey began, before I knew what it would become. Now that it's in progress, it's becoming evident that I was right: this is an adventure. Before each day begins I have an idea what's about to happen, but that morphs as soon as it happens, which is what adventure is all about.

I recall reading about how psychiatric wards used to have garden mazes, labyrinths, where you walked into the garden, the green maze, and got lost. But you weren't really lost, because you knew there was a way out. There was a path, and all you had to do was discover it. In fact, the difference between a labyrinth and a maze is that, in a labyrinth, there is only one entrance and one exit, and only one way to get from one to the other. Mental institutions used garden labyrinths as a tool for mental health, because life is like a labyrinth. We don't know exactly where we're going, but we have an idea of the direction. Reading the maps in the map case on the handlebar bag of my bike makes me feel as if I'm in a labyrinth. I have an idea where I am, and where I'm going, but I've never been here before.

The twins I met are not using maps. Their path to biking adventure involves not knowing what lies beyond the next bend. When I went over Sherman pass, I knew that I was going to climb 5,000 feet; they didn't. For them, it was discovery. What I experience that they do not is roads best suited for bicyclists, roadways recommended by the Adventure Cycling Association, old highways that run parallel to the new highways. I'm glad I leverage the maps, but they come at a price. They tell me where I'm going.

Once when I was pursuing a Master of Fine Arts in creative writing at the University of Alaska, Fairbanks, I heard the short-story writer Rick Bass give a craft talk. The essence of his talk was that every time you get something, you give something up. He used the Wright Brothers as an example. When they took off at Kitty Hawk, mankind learned how to fly—but all the birds lost their power. Imagine what mankind saw when they observed birds fly before we created flight technology. That day altered us forever. This is not a knock on the technology of flying; the trip I'm taking would not have been possible had I not flown to Seattle so I could bike back to Milwaukee. It just seems relevant to acknowledge what we lose when we acquire great leaps in technology. The maps I leverage are a form of technology; they tell me where to go. Without the maps, I would share a similar experience to that of the twins: having an idea of what's next but not knowing exactly what that is.

I thought I'd meet more bicycle tourists my age on this ride, but so far they're all in their twenties. Most of them recently graduated from college and are going for long bike rides before starting their careers. When I graduated with a bachelor's degree in English, I did something similar. I worked as a furniture delivery driver for nine months and saved every penny, so I could travel through Europe for five months. I had guidebooks; there was a plan as to which countries I'd visit and how I'd travel about. But one of the goals was to do something like what I'm doing now: to live minimally. To try to spend as little as possible under the assumption that the less you spend, the more adventure you have. I found that to be so true that, when the trip was over, I went back to driving the furniture delivery truck for another six months so I could have another adventure backpacking through Southeast Asia.

What surprises me is that I'm re-experiencing now the sense of discovery that I felt then. Thirty years down the road, it's still possible to find wonder in the unknown.

Back then, the hardest part about traveling for months at a time was being away from my girlfriend, Sue. Now, after 25 years of marriage to her, I experience the same dilemma. I love being on an adventure, but I miss her. We talk and email daily, but technology doesn't make up for physical presence. I know it's easier for me than it is for her, because I'm the one on the adventure. This knowledge comes at a price: I love her more than I did then, so much more, and the more I love her, the harder it is to be away on an adventure.

This is why I love Sue. Neither of us has many friends, because we prefer each other's company. I spend time alone, I spend time with Sue, and I spend time with Kait and Evan. Sue enabled me to embrace introversion, and I love her for it. It goes without saying that Sue and I know each other. We're talking on the phone twice a day while I'm on this trip, so we can stay abreast of what's happening in each other's lives. I'm going to be away from her only for a month, yet so much can happen in a month. Certainly a great deal is happening to me on this journey, and I want to keep her up to date on what I'm learning, so I don't overwhelm her when I return.

I have a list of morals that dictate my conduct, and one of them is: "Love your wife, then love your children, then love everyone else." Sue comes first; yet here I am, biking through Idaho all by myself.

MONTANA

DAY EIGHT

I had a lot of fun shopping for the stuff I brought on this trip. My favorite purchase is a product made by Therm-a-Rest: you place your inflatable sleeping pad into it, click a few straps together, and suddenly your sleeping pad is converted into a lounge chair. Brilliant.

I'm sitting in the lounge chair now, inside my one-person tent, sitting out a thunderstorm. It was a tiring day. After leaving Spirit Lake, I caught a tailwind that brought me into Sandpoint at a quick pace. When I rolled into town, I looked down to discover another flat. That made four flats in eight days, all from the same tire. I had called Kevin at Outdoor Experience, a bike shop in Sandpoint, and asked him to hold a couple of tubes for me, since the size of the bike's rims is unusual. Kevin had the tubes, and he also had a sweet pair of Continental touring tires that I bought from him as well.

When I was paying for the supplies, Kevin offered some good advice: "Don't rush it between here and East Glacier. Look around. There's plenty of time in the Great Plains to make up big miles." He told me this because he's seen plenty of bike riders in a hurry to put miles on the road, which is not necessarily a good idea when you're biking through some of the most breathtaking country available. I do have distance goals; I need to make it back to Milwaukee by mid-August. But maybe I can learn from Kevin and wait to worry about making up miles when riding the straight roads of eastern Montana and North Dakota.

Ten miles east of Sandpoint, I met a cycling couple heading the other direction. They are in their seventies and started their journey in Bar Harbor, Maine. A farming couple from Iowa spending their retirement years bike touring. How beautiful is that?

I was able to watch the thunderstorm develop as the day progressed. Studying the map, I decided to camp at a Kootenai National Forest campground that borders the Cabinet Gorge Reservoir. Because I ended the ride in the early afternoon, I had time to take a swim in the lake and prepare dinner before the thunder and ensuing rain arrived. It also gives me some additional hours to sit in this tent, an activity I'm now fond of. I can hear the wind in the trees and the rain hitting the tent, but I can't see it. After a day on the bike, riding through more mountains and along more rivers, it's good to dial back the sensory intake.

Yesterday I mentioned that I have a list of morals that dictate my conduct, and that one of them is: "Love your wife, then your children, then everyone else." I have such a list of morals as a result of teaching Ethics at the university. I learned quickly that few of my students have guiding principles in their lives. When I asked what principles they would turn to in order to help determine how they should behave, some mentioned the Golden Rule: Do unto others as you would have them do unto you. Others would mention the Ten Commandments. But when I asked them if they honestly used these ethical principles on a daily basis, to help them determine not just what they do but how they do it, they said no.

That created an in-class activity that was both surprising and powerful. I asked the students to make up their own lists of ethical concepts that would directly connect to their personal conduct. After all, I told them, what is the point of having ethics if they don't help you do what you should do? The students were excited at the prospect of this activity—until they tried doing it. They found it extremely difficult, because they first had to come to terms with the fact that they had no ethics per se. Yes, they had role models that they looked to for modeled behavior, and yes, they had faith communities that provided guidance and direction. But the information they were handed was so general that it was difficult for them to connect it to their day-to-day decision-making process. Yet creating customized, specified ethical principles also seemed beyond their grasp.

So I picked up a piece of chalk and told them I'd do it first. I also found it difficult, though not impossible. I came up with the following:

1. Love your wife, then your children, then everyone else

2. Slowness (serenity)

3. Non-thought (mental autonomy)

4. Solitude (spend as much time alone as possible)

5. Impermanence

6. Controlled risk (adventure)

It took the rest of the quarter for me to explain these principles, but doing so helped my students, and myself, come to terms with personalized ethics.

I explained how loving my kids is an extension of loving Sue, but it's important that the kids understand that she is the most important person in my life—that their mother is important. We have a tight nuclear family. Even though Kait goes to school in Minnesota, and Evan aspires to study in Oregon, we're a team. Having this ethic—family first, and wife above all—ensures that my actions support this principle. Even though this bike ride takes me away from them, I believe it will help the family dynamic. I'm just not sure how yet.

I've already discussed the ethic of "slow." This trip certainly supports that practice, although I have to remind myself. Even today, I caught myself worrying about the distance to the next turn, my overall speed, if my legs could handle the day's ride. My goal for tomorrow is to go slower than I did today. I equate serenity, or peace of mind, with slowness. I hope I have the presence of mind to know when I need to dial it back on the bike so I can be more aware of what I'm doing.

That's all I want to cover today. The other ethical principles involve a great deal of thought, and I'm not up to it. I lost an hour now that we're in Mountain Time. I'm not exactly sure what that means, losing an hour. I'll wake up tomorrow at the same time I did yesterday.

One final thought. It was difficult to leave Suzanne and Denny's cabin. I've been there several times before. It's familiar. I knew where to find the dishware, already had my favorite couch, knew before I took a shower that the pressure would be forceful. It was nice to be somewhere familiar for a day. It was restful. Adventure is not restful. Adventure is not exactly knowing what comes next.

DAY NINE

Last week, I was in a morning rush to get on the road and beat the heat and traffic. Then I enjoyed two slow mornings at Suzanne and Denny's cabin. Something must have left a mark, because I'm not busting out of camp on this beautiful Montana morning. Fortunately there is cell coverage here, so I had a good half-hour phone call with Sue while making hot coffee over the Optimus. Then a peanut butter and jam wrap for breakfast.

The sky is overcast, and I'm sure to hit rain today, so why hurry it along? Learn a lesson from Kevin at the bike shop and look around. Be in the space, rather than just passing through it. I'm sure I'll still get a good eighty miles in on the bike today, just not all at once, and not all in the morning.

The personal "moral principles" I created that day in class—I keep a copy of them on a laminated card in my wallet. I take out the card and review them when I need guidance with a given decision on how to conduct myself. That doesn't happen very often, but often enough to justify the process.

I think that's how people end up doing bad things: they have no guiding principles to turn to. I haven't met many people who are intentionally "bad" or "evil." I think most bad choices are the result of a lack of moral direction.

I'm lucky in that I teach an Ethics class. I get to see how my own ethics and behavior change from year to year. I'll update the list of moral principles when learning about new topics that are important enough to make the list. For example, when I was doing Ironman, I had this moral: "harden the fuck up," or HTFU. It's a phrase I learned from an Australian triathlete on a triathlon discussion forum, and it basically means "suck it up and get to it." It's interesting, because HTFU left a mark on me; it's that attitude that I'm trying to combat right now. Now I strive not for speed but for slowness. It's no longer about hardening up; it's now about looking around as you roll down the road.

The third moral principle is non-thought. Abe Masao was one of Nishida's students. Here is his take on Zen Buddhism and non-thought:

> Zen does not establish itself on the basis of either thinking or not-thinking, but rather non-thinking, which is beyond both thinking and not-thinking. When not-thinking is taken as the basis of Zen, anti-intellectualism becomes rampant. When thinking is taken as the basis, Zen loses its authentic ground and degenerates into mere conceptualism and abstract verbiage. Genuine Zen, however, takes non-thinking as its ultimate ground, and thus can express itself without hindrance through both thinking and not-thinking, as the situation requires.

It's difficult for Westerners to come to terms with this concept of non-thought, or at least it is for my students when I try talking about it in Creative Thinking classes. To help them out, I break it down into three categories:

1. Thought: when your mind creates thought in a logical sequence for a logical purpose.

2. Non-thought: when your mind is active but not logically focused, is spontaneous, is active yet not directed.

3. Not thinking: when you're watching reruns of The Simpsons.

In Western culture, meditation is a loaded term. But I think that, when done right, it mirrors this concept of non-thought. You may be focusing on a mantra or a spot on the wall in order to let your mind focus on something, but you don't let your mind run rampant with thought.

That's why I like Nishida's sense of Pure Experience, which to me seems like "meditation in motion." I can illustrate this with a cycling analogy:

1. Cycling: when you focus on the map to figure out where you need to turn next, check your mirror for traffic, look at your computer to see how fast you're going, etc.

2. Non-cycling: when you are so engaged in the activity of cycling that an hour or two can go by, and you're pretty much unaware of it. You're that engaged in the activity. Your mind is active, but you're not managing it with logistical details.

3. Not cycling: when you're on the couch, watching reruns of The Simpsons.

The more I engage a state of non-thought, the easier it is for me to do things like bike over mountain passes. I'm not thinking about what I'm doing; I'm just doing.

Now it's the end of the day, and I'm in yet another Montana Forest Service campground, 85 miles closer to my destination. It was a great day of riding, because I kept thinking about Kevin's advice: enjoy Montana while you're here. I did hit my mileage goal for the day, but I tried hard to slow down the pace of the bike. As long as I was keeping it over 10 mph, I was doing okay. The slow speeds going up were compensated by the quick descents.

Along the way, I ran into a couple on a motorcycle. Not just any motorcycle, but a 1980s-era BMW R100. They had a flat, and their cell coverage didn't reach where they were, so they weren't sure what to do. I tried my mobile phone, and fortunately my carrier provided service. Problem solved: they got on the phone to their friend in Troy for help. It felt great to finally help someone out, in light of how many people have helped me already on this trip.

The Adventure Cycling Association maps don't take me on the most direct routes, but they do provide roads that are relatively free of traffic and rich in scenery. Frequently I see hawks or a three-point buck drinking from a stream, hear crickets so loud they would frighten me. All this life around me, and little visible human impact.

My fourth moral principle, "solitude," is a good fit for this landscape. I met new people often last week, but at Suzanne and Denny's cabin I was all by myself, and I've been pretty much alone since then, opting to camp solo. There are the phone calls to Sue and the email correspondence when I find wi-fi—which, surprisingly, has happened every day so far. But in terms of physical solitude, I have it.

When I'm at home or at work, I make a concerted effort to be alone when I can. I like being a professor because you teach a couple of classes a day, and you have the perfunctory meetings to go to, but the rest of the time it's just you and your office. You grade papers, respond to emails, read theory, and you're all alone. It's a great career for an introvert.

I also think that spending time alone enhances the time I spend with people. If I've been alone enough, then I have plenty of energy for listening and talking to people. I don't care much for small talk, so I tend to get to the point of the matter rather quickly. And if I don't do that because the person I'm engaging does, then I just listen. But I want to listen actively, to let that person know I'm paying close attention to what he or she has to say. I like to learn, so this seems to be the best way to learn from other human beings. Throw in some effective non-verbal gestures such as good eye contact and a few nods of the head, and you have a great discussion taking place.

But it takes energy, and I can do it for only so long. I love to teach, but an hour with the students requires at least two hours in my office to recuperate. The same can be said with friends and family: if we have guests over for dinner we usually have a great time, but when the guests leave, we clean up and go straight to bed. We're exhausted.

So that's why I'm into solitude. That's why I didn't want to do this bike ride with someone else. I enjoy who I am, I enjoy my own company, and I create opportunities to be alone.

DAY TEN

It's almost eleven in the morning, and I'm at a coffee shop on the side of the highway running through Eureka. I've already put about 45 miles on the bike. Woke up around five-thirty and was on the road by six. The morning hours are pure magic. The light, the aroma: pastoral intoxication. Western Montana is like no other place I've been before. The sheer scale, the magnitude of the entire landscape does things to the mind and spirit. It's humbling.

The first 30 miles paralleled the reservoir, so the road would go up for long stretches and then down. My legs were pretty heavy this morning after yesterday's ride; I started to wonder if I was happy this morning, climbing up and up. Of course I was. It was just a matter of reminding myself that happiness was present.

Then I reflected on those times in my life when the metaphorical road just kept going up and up: when I was trying to finish my doctoral dissertation, when I worked for Microsoft. Those challenging times in life that seemed never to end. I was not happy then, not the way I'm happy now. I knew about Nishida and his pure experience, but only in theory. I knew of non-thought, but thoughts clouded my mind like a Montana thundercloud.

I know people who work hard every day of their lives and exhibit happiness; I know more people who work hard every day and do not. Maybe that's why I'm somewhat selective as to whom I spend time with, because of the influence they can have on my happiness. If I like to work hard, and if that work makes me happy, then let me work with those who feel the same way. As for those who don't, I still work with them but not to the same depth.

I also know those whose metaphorical road just keeps going down—one big descent into pleasure. The pantheistic hedonists. My undergraduate college experience was like this. I tend to do things to an extreme, so when I wanted to introduce myself to pleasure, it was extreme. Partying on water-towers, skiing off cliffs, racing around on a motorcycle. I was named the "Dionysian Fool" of my graduating class, a yearly award handed out by the student body government to recognize the most metaphysically dangerous graduate. It was all a new type of intoxication. But it didn't lead to happiness.

I was an English major at the time. English was a great degree program, because it meant I didn't have to take any exams. All you had to do was write essays, and I could get help from friends with that whenever I needed it. Not a bad deal, but it didn't help me when I landed in graduate school, where I had to do the real work of essay writing without much individual experience at it. Eventually, all that pursuit of pleasure at the expense of doing the work catches up to you.

So far, the experience of the bicycle on this trip has been a steady blend of happiness and pleasure. You go up (happiness), and then you go down (pleasure). There's not much flat land in this part of the world. It will be interesting to see if the different topography of the Great Plains alters that.

The fifth moral principle is impermanence. It's not hard to explain: everything organic ends. I find this moral extremely helpful when things end: when people die, when pets die, whenever I lose something or someone I care about.

I'm one of those guys who develop a strong relationship with certain physical objects. My bikes, for example: I care a great deal about them, and as a result I have a hard time sharing them. I used to have a single-speed Schwinn track bike that my friend Mark got me at a sweet price. I loved riding that bike to work and back. And, because it wasn't grandiose, no one thought about stealing it when it was locked up in downtown Milwaukee. I took that bike everywhere. I shared the bike with Evan, because he loved riding the single-speed too. It's truly the best bike for a flat Midwestern city like Milwaukee. But there came the day when Evan tacoed the rear rim. He didn't know how it happened; it just happened. I looked at the bike, and I looked at him, and I said, "Well, that's the impermanence of the universe." This was one of the best moments I can think of, in terms of raising Evan. He knew I loved that bike, and he did not want to tell me that he had wrecked it. But he did, and I returned his honesty by acknowledging that he was worth much more to me than the bike was.

It may seem obvious that a father should value his son over his bicycle. But with me that's not always the case. I love my stuff; I take very good care of my stuff. Which is why I need a moral principle of impermanence, to keep me in check when I give priority to the tangible over the intangible.

And I wasn't able to replace the rim, so I had to get a new, and better, single-speed bike. Lovely impermanence.

Of course, there is life's impermanence. On my twenty-first birthday, I was bicycling to work on East Marginal Way south of Seattle. I was paying close attention to the semi-trucks rolling by within inches of me, when suddenly I crossed a railroad track that was at a 45-degree angle to the road. My front tire got caught in the track, and I started to fall into the road just as a semi was hugging me. I was lucky: when I hit the ground between the wheels of the semi's trailer, I bounced up just enough so that, when its rear tires hit me, they propelled me twenty feet onto the side of the road, rather than run me over. The trip to the hospital in an ambulance was full of medical people telling me how lucky I was to be alive.

I'm lucky to be alive. I wasn't able to get back on a bike for two years, I was so afraid of getting hit again. But I did get back in the saddle, gradually, on trails at first, then on roads. Biking is a way of living. There are risks, and there is impermanence.

The final moral is "controlled risk," with an emphasis on adventure. It's a concept I learned from motorcycle school, because riding a motorcycle is inherently risky, so you learn how to ride it as best you can in order to control the risk. You learn how to do a late apex going into a turn. You learn to check your mirrors every five seconds. You learn to stay at least two seconds behind the vehicle in front of you. Controlled risk.

The better you know how to control the motorcycle, the more you can risk. There are limits to controlled risk, limits that my friends and family would remind me of on a regular basis, which is why, to the great pleasure of my wife, I sold the motorcycle last year. That doesn't mean that life's adventure ended; I've simply transferred it, at this moment, into bicycle touring. The risk was in making the transition from motorcycle touring to bicycle touring, without having experienced the adventure of bicycle touring before. So far, ten days into this adventure, I'm happy to say that the exchange is paying off.

I think it's risky not to engage in risk. I don't want to have regret. I want to experience life. When a logging truck passes me on a road with no shoulder, I feel the risk—and I feel alive. Of course, the risk is controlled. A few times, when I've seen the truck coming at me in my handlebar mirror, I've just pulled off to the side of the road and let him pass. That's the control.

You can't control everything in life. Trying to do so minimizes the chance of adventure. And sometimes the risk will eventually catch up to you and bite you in the ass. But I'm okay with that. It's how I want to live. It's why my sixth and final moral principle is controlled risk.

DAY ELEVEN

I pulled into Whitefish in the midst of road construction: dump trucks, gravel trucks, pickup trucks. The road was ripped up coming into town, and it was raining, so mud got all over me and the bike.

I wasn't the only cyclist pulling into town. I caught up to four cyclists riding two tandems: a mom and her young son on the back and a father with their very young daughter. Both bikes were loaded with gear. Like me, they were all covered in mud. The kids looked to be enjoying the muddy moment. We had to stop periodically for the roadwork to commence, which gave us a chance to chat. They are a cycling family. The mom and dad are both Seattle school teachers, so every summer the four of them take off on a grand bicycling adventure. This is the biggest journey so far, going from Seattle to Glacier National Park. They'll take the train back. The kids said they are pretty ready to see the park.

My first stop in town was at the local bike shop, Glacier Cyclery. I wanted to get the Salsa checked out one last time before crossing the Plains. There won't be another proper bike shop until Bismarck, and that's a couple of weeks away.

As I rolled up to the shop, the owner stepped out and said, "You look filthy. We better hose you and your bike off!" So to the back of the building we went to wash the mud and dirt off me and the Salsa. I then rolled it into their shop so they could look it over. All was fine, but they did adjust the brake and shifter cables, which had stretched from the use they had received over the last ten days.

I was also able to purchase two new tubes and a tire gauge. I think my tire troubles are over, but it's good to be prepared. I also bought a fluorescent yellow vest. Most bike tourers I've seen wear some type of fluorescent clothing. It makes sense: be seen, be safe.

While waiting for the bike I called Meg, a friend of Suzanne and Denny's with whom Denny put me in touch several weeks ago. Meg and her husband Steve live in Whitefish and agreed to host me for the night, if I agreed to tell them all about the trip. Meg offered to ride her bike to the bike shop so we could bike back to her home together. When she arrived, I was talking to four other cyclists who had just rolled into town and couldn't find a place to stay. They asked me where I was staying, and I told them. At which point Meg said, "Why don't you come along too?" They did, and we had a great evening together over beers and dinner, telling stories of the journeys we were on.

I confessed that I wasn't sure I would have invited five people I didn't know to my home. We then had a conversation about the nature of generosity and hospitality, how you can be open to it or not. The other cyclists told of similar experiences they've had while biking down the road. This generosity constant is certainly not limited to my experience. It seems to be available to those who are available to it.

I was thinking of the twins and how their biking method involves stealth camping: throwing your gear down in an inauspicious place for the night, then waking early and heading on down the road. Stealth camping works for what the twins want to get from their experience. I'm just glad that I know Denny and Suzanne, and that they know Meg and Steve, and that all these people are willing to share their homes and hospitality.

I keep reflecting on how I want to believe in humanity, how I want to think better of people. I'm not a big fan of our species; I've seen a lot of selfish behavior in my life, and it makes me want to disconnect gradually and do my own thing. Meeting generous people is changing that. I'm becoming a believer, and I think the best way to learn how to believe in basic human goodness is to meet people who are basically good.

DAY TWELVE

I'm in Glacier National Park. It was a short two-hour ride to get from Meg and Steve's house to here. The ACA maps took me on some back highway that turned into a back road that turned into gravel. It's the first "A" in "ACA" that makes the maps interesting.

At the Visitor's Center in the park I ran into a cyclist on a tandem named Gary. Gary had just been offered some bear spray by a stranger who no longer needed it, since he was leaving the park. Gary didn't need it because he already had a can of bear spray, so he offered it to me, and I gladly accepted it. You can't be too careful when it comes to bears in this part of Montana, and on a bicycle you're rather exposed to bears. I asked Gary who was riding on the tandem with him, and he said, "No one. It's a tribute ride for my wife, who died two years ago from pancreatic cancer."

This caught me by surprise; all I could say was "I'm sorry for your loss," for which he thanked me. Like me, Gary had shipped his bike to Seattle and started his ride there. And, also like me, he's stopping at Lake Michigan, since he lives in Traverse City. But unlike me, he's riding for a cause, a tribute. The road into the park doesn't open for cyclists until four o'clock so cyclists don't get into the thick of the automobile and RV traffic, so we'll leave for Avalanche Campground then. I hope we camp in the same place tonight.

Gary told me that it's hard being without his wife, and he's just trying to be grateful for the 35 years they had together. I didn't know what to say. Like Gary, I'm deeply in love with my wife, but mine is waiting for me back in Wisconsin. All I could do was listen to Gary tell me how much he loves his deceased wife.

At four o'clock, I biked with Gary in a deluge of rain to Avalanche, the last campsite before the ascent to Logan Pass. Following his tandem, I couldn't help but imagine his wife on the back. About halfway to Avalanche the rain subsided, so we stopped to check out a series of waterfalls. A couple approached Gary and asked him who was riding on the tandem with him, so he proceeded to tell them that his bike ride was a tribute for his wife, "who died two years ago from pancreatic cancer." It was the same message he shared with me, almost word for word, and as I listened to him retell his story, I wondered how many times a day he was asked the question.

We arrived at the campsite to find Dave from Moscow, Idaho. Dave and Gary met at a bike hostel in Washington, and they've been crossing each other's paths ever since. We stood beneath the tall evergreens, trying to stay dry as it rained and hailed.

We had to register for the campsite, so I offered to deposit all of our fees and save the others from having to go into the rain and darkness. After I found the payment station, it began raining in sheets, so I stood under the station's awning, listening and watching the rain, waiting for it to end.

Then kindness found me again. The family camping next to the awning must have seen me trying to wait out the rain, because they invited me to join them for dinner. Maguy, Phil, and Phil, a family having their yearly vacation in the park. We enjoyed chicken and mashed potatoes; it's cliché to say that food always tastes better when you're camping, but it tastes fantastic when you're camping in the rain and the four of you are huddled around a picnic table beneath a blue tarp. I told them that all I could offer in exchange for the meal was a story, so I told them about my wife and how much I love her and my two children.

When our conversation and meal ended, I thanked them and returned to the campsite. It was still raining hard. A guy from the next campsite approached with a bundle of wood, dry paper, and matches, and offered them to us. He thought we could use a fire because we looked cold. His name was Adam, and he was right; a day of bicycling in the rain makes a deep chill. We graciously accepted the wood, and Dave, whose career was in the Forest Service, made a fire in less than five minutes. Soon we were standing in the warmth of the fire, drinking beer, wine, and bourbon, exchanging stories of the day's ride.

DAY THIRTEEN

By nine in the morning I had summited Logan Pass, elevation 6,646 feet. I had no idea why it was so cold up there, 42 degrees, in mid-July. The happiness I experienced climbing Sherman Pass is back. The ride from the campground to the summit was sixteen miles of happiness, stopping periodically to take in the view. I had the entire road, the entire park, to myself. Last night when we were drinking around the campfire, a ranger came and joined in our conversation. He told us that the number of visitors to the park has increased 29 percent this year, and that it had increased 24 percent the year before that. So many cars and RVs—but the number of people is dwarfed by the sheer scale of this national park.

I cannot describe the scale of the mountains. I learned long ago the limits to language. As hard as I could try to describe what this looks like, I would fail, because words are merely symbols of what is real. Many have tried, but a description of the mountain is a representation, not the mountain itself.

The descent down Logan Pass was a ride through the rain. The temps were cold, and the bike has developed a wobble when it exceeds 23 miles per hour. I pulled over and adjusted the headset and tried adjusting the load in the panniers, but the wobble persisted. I also stopped to look at one of the glaciers. Glacier recession models predict that all the glaciers in the park will melt by 2030. I'm glad I saw them; it's probably my last chance to do so.

It was good to arrive at St. Mary's. I pulled into the campground, paid the ranger for the site, went to the bike-specific site, pitched the tent, rode into town, found a restaurant, and had a bacon cheeseburger and two beers.

When you're outside for days on end, you begin to appreciate the indoors. When I'm at home, I do all I can to spend time outside. Outside is now too much of a good thing.

I'm in the tent at the campground and just took a two-hour nap. It's going to rain all afternoon, so this is the best way to avoid getting wet. A couple of weeks ago, I wouldn't have had the patience to sit in a tent and listen to the rain.

Dave from Idaho is in the same campsite. His tent is staked five feet from mine, so we're having an ongoing conversation, which is odd since we are in separate tents. He found a copy of *The Hungry Horse News*, the local newspaper. When he was done reading it from front to back, he shared it with me, so now we're chatting about what is newsworthy in this part of the country:

- "At about 9 a.m. Jamie Brandon, 34, allegedly stole a green Subaru Legacy from an unlocked garage on 2nd Avenue East in Columbia Falls. The vehicle was unlocked and the keys were not inside. Two hours later Brandon caused an accident in Whitefish. He was charged with theft and burglary."

- "A man reported that a package with clothing and household items was stolen two months ago from his front porch on Riparian Drive. He tried to track it down first before reporting it stolen."

- "A mountain lion wandered into a backyard on 4th Avenue West. Two men with guns planned to shoot the animal, but police persuaded them to go home. As did the cat, going back into the bushes."

Waking early this morning and riding up Logan Pass took some effort. The road is narrow, and the drop from the road is straight down in places. I think you feel it more on a bicycle than in a car, since a bike has no exoskeleton: it's just you, the stone wall, and the drop. So much snow in the mountains in July. No wonder you can go over this pass only during two or three months of the year.

Earlier, I was reflecting on the quality of people you spend time with. To find "the good," it helps to work and live with people who are good. But of course, we don't always have the opportunity to be surrounded by good people.

You typically don't get to pick who you work with. I advise my students who are about to graduate to consider not just what kind of work they are going to do, but who they are going to do it for and with. My thirty years of professional experience have taught me that who you work for is as important as what you do, if not more important. You may choose a job because of its description, but you typically leave it because you don't get along with the people. Some people are givers; some are takers. My career over the last few years has been a strange blend of the two. I've had to make sure that they didn't take something from me that I couldn't get back.

During my tech years, it was the boom time for startup companies in Seattle, and there was a wealth of opportunities for someone who could learn quickly and embrace new technology. I needed the work, because my six-month student loan deferment was about to close. On top of that, Sue told me that she was pregnant with our second child. We had a new mini-farm and too many mouths to feed: a couple of horses, a pony, three dogs, five cats, one girl, and a boy on the way. Making an income was suddenly the primary objective in my life.

Finding work wasn't easy. I had two terminal degrees but no transferable work experience. In job interviews, I could talk up a storm about rhetorical theory, but I couldn't draft a specification document or a business proposal. I loved to write, but the jobs I interviewed for were for positions where it didn't matter whether you loved writing essays and poems. You just had to write copious amounts of technically dense copy. I didn't much care for that, but I did care about securing gainful employment.

Then I got lucky. I interviewed for a small startup called Health Knowledge. They wanted to create an intranet that would securely share confidential medical information among hospitals, clinics, and insurance providers—a brilliant idea that was much needed but did not yet exist. The woman who interviewed me was Jane Bedinger, the Web Services Director for Product Marketing.

From where I was sitting, the job interview wasn't going well, because all we talked about was the poplar tree blowing outside the window of her office. After ten minutes of that, I figured she had probably offered the job to the person who interviewed before me, because we were not discussing my resume. So, I simply enjoyed the conversation. The talk about the tree's dollar-sized leaves led to a discussion about Li Po and Tu Fu, two of my favorite Japanese poets. And that led to a brief discussion about our mutual admiration for punctuation—the power of the n-dash, the common cultural abuse of misappropriated commas. And at the end of the interview, to my great surprise, Jane offered me the job on a contract-to-hire basis: I would work as a contractor for three months, and then we would talk about the possibility of my interviewing again for a full-time position.

I was both ecstatic and confused. I was able to go home and tell Sue that I had landed a job. It wasn't full-time, but it was income. But I was confused because the interview had had nothing to do with work per se. I didn't dwell on that, so happy was I to have a job to go to the following Monday.

After contracting for three months, I did interview with Jane for a full-time position. When I walked into her office to interview, I jokingly said that I hoped this interview wouldn't be like the last one, because all we had talked about then was trees and poetry.

Jane laughed, then told me that her method was intentional: "In an hour's time, I had to discern if you were someone who would work well with my team, as well as someone I want to work with." She said she could tell by my resume that I was professionally proficient, and what I didn't know technologically she could teach me. What she couldn't teach me was how to listen or how to react to ideas in real time, those soft skills that take years to engender. I'll never forget those two interviews, not just because they ended with employment opportunities, but because they taught me that Jane would be the best manager I'd ever have.

I did work well with her team, because she hired good people I could share ideas with. It wasn't about my intellectual contribution to the company; it was about the team's intellectual contributions.

Jane made me want to work hard, because I wanted Jane to look good in the eyes of the c-level executives. Jane invested in me. She sent me to trainings. She let our weekly meetings go on for hours as we talked about the direction of the team's projects. She would not answer the phone or check email while we met. She made me, just one of her many employees, a priority.

Two years later, Jane left the company to start a consulting firm. The company wasn't the same without her, so I opted to jump ship and take a contracting job at Microsoft. I should have known from the interview—a phone interview lasting all of twenty minutes— that I wouldn't like the job I was offered, because all we talked about was what Jane had opted not to talk about: my resume and technical skills.

It wasn't a good time to work for Microsoft. Their stock was high, so people were working there just so they could eventually cash out their stock options. It was less about the work than about the end reward. It's not fair to compare my Microsoft managers to Jane Bedinger. It was a completely different work environment, with completely different people, focusing on an entirely different set of goals. My group's ultimate goal was to build an advertising engine that would allow MSN, their public Internet space, to push two million ads a day. I thought the problem was interesting from a technological perspective but not from a moral perspective, because Web space should be about more than viewing ads and designing a back-end technology that mined data on users based on their tracked Internet surfing habits.

I learned a great deal working at Microsoft, but I can't say that everything I learned was good. Microsoft taught me how to work for ten hours a day, drive home, open my laptop, and work some more. Microsoft taught me how to pay closer attention to the company's stock value than to its core mission statement. It taught me how to laugh at colleagues who made public mistakes and to take pleasure in their professional humiliation.

The manager I reported to was a technological genius, but her communication skills were nearly nonexistent. She did not know how to run a meeting, let alone conduct a conversation. She valued her people in regard to the deliverables we could build. I was learning under her management, but I was not growing.

Our group was successful; we were building a great advertising engine. But it was so successful that other leadership in the company wanted to take it over in time for the product launch, so they fired our leaders and reorganized the entire team, a process that took six months, during which I had nothing to do, because the future direction of my deliverables was in stasis. My manager told me to act busy and look like I was getting things done. All that led to was hours upon hours of Internet surfing. I grew bored of that, so I quit.

It took me years to unlearn what I had learned at Microsoft, not in terms of technical skills but in terms of how people should be treated.

DAY FOURTEEN

I'm on the side of the road in central Montana, watching a rancher herd his cattle. The east side of Glacier National Park is in the background, my last view of mountains. The landscape's sudden transition from majestic mountains to Great Plains is startling. In an hour's time riding the bike, the world has shifted.

The weather system that made me hole up in my tent yesterday isn't going away; it's staying near the mountains. The route I intended to take through Canada hugs the park, and I don't need two more days like yesterday. I need sunshine and tailwind, so it looks like I won't be leaving Montana quite yet. I'll take the route south to Cut Bank and try for Shelby by evening. That's about 85 miles due east, a good day of cycling.

I'm still contemplating the nuances of happiness. I climbed the five mountain passes and enjoyed each one. Now that there are no more mountains to climb, now that I'm heading into the Great Plains, will I still be as happy? Is happiness in proportion to the challenge that comes with it? Crossing eastern Montana and North Dakota will be a challenge, but a different challenge with a different type of happiness.

The Salsa suddenly feels less like a pack mule and more like a quarter horse.

I made it to Shelby by four in the afternoon. There was a slight tailwind, and I took advantage of it. Today is my birthday, so I gave myself a stay at the Sherlock Hotel. It's my favorite type of hotel, the kind that has the room's door facing the parking lot. The room has everything I need: a shower, a sink to do laundry in, racks to hang my tent on so it can dry out from last night's rain, outlets to recharge the laptop, phone, and camera. And a bed. I haven't showered in days, and I haven't slept well in the tent, so tonight is going to be a sweet birthday treat.

The hotel room also offers solitude. It's my first hotel stay on this trip. I've had showers and access to laundry facilities through the Warm Showers network. It's a great resource for bicycle travelers, but it comes with an obligation to interact with your hosts. I do enjoy that, but having a small hotel room in a small Montana railroad town all to myself is just the gift I wanted.

I began this trip focusing on the struggle of loving my wife and also loving solitude. At the start, I was focused on solitude; now that I'm biking through the Great Plains, I find myself thinking of Sue. It could be that the mountains were simply a sensory overload; every time you round a bend, a new panorama offered itself. The Great Plains are different, more of a reoccurring theme. It's as much of a mental shift as it is a transition of topography. Now that the land is rolling, I'm thinking differently. In place of thunderheads, endless puffs of clouds. What was vertical has become horizontal. And at the edge of the horizon is Sue.

Sue and I once lived in this kind of landscape, the Palouse of Eastern Washington. She was getting her veterinary degree, I was pursuing my Ph.D., and we were remodeling an old farm house we could not have afforded if it had not been for student loans. We leveraged those loans to purchase the house as well as a truck, a horse trailer, and two horses. Sue grew up with horses, and having them in the paddock served as a stress release from veterinary school. She loved the horses, Presley and Review. I was invested in her happiness, so the horses became an important part of our lives.

We were so poor, yet we had horses. We had our first child while we had horses.

This part of central Montana is horse country. I ride down Highway 2, and horses run away when they hear me. They have all the space to run that they could want. Miles of land full of horses running away from a cyclist.

I cleaned up after our horses and worked on the horse stalls. It was good labor. I never made a connection with Presley and Review the way Sue did, but they were a resource for the poetry I wrote at the time. I wanted to understand why Sue loved those horses so much, when I did not. One of my own favorite poems came from trying to understand that struggle.

In Sixteen Hands of Shadow

How does one prepare for those
moments when death approaches easily and without asking?

We walk the horses to the field not
knowing the neighbor rolled his old red
truck onto the edge of the trail.
We turn the bend.
The roan sees the red and propels
sideways and through you and
for seconds four hooves dance about your head.
Somehow he does not touch you.
From the ground, amidst his dance, all you see
is my fear. Your sudden comforting,
brushing yourself and telling me he loves you
as much as I do,
its just that color he's unsure of. You hold me,
tell me there is nothing in nature as red as that truck,
nothing so large and solid in this color. You remind
me that there is nothing as wonderful as the unknown
power resting in the eye of a horse.

In such moments, when you try to help me understand why,
I must trust what reflects the eye,
ray retracting your pupil, darkness filling with dark
brown, or blood dripping from your lip bitten in
fear of the horse's hooves landing
on your fallen body, blood lifting through
the lip with each smile, taste of blood in a kiss.

The poem reminds me how I loved Sue, a different type of love than
I have for her now. Our love then was fresh and dramatic. Over the
years, it has matured to include the experiences of raising children,
establishing careers, going on vacations and, best of all, the day-
to-day boring details we've shared for 25 years. There's some life-
threatening drama in the poem; you don't get that in the decades of
daily life we've experienced. Or there is drama, but you have to look
closer to find it.

DAY FIFTEEN

I'm making good time today. Its noon, and I've already put in 60 miles. I was hoping to camp at the Fairgrounds in Havre, but they aren't hosting bike campers tonight because it's the last night of the county fair. Maybe I won't worry about where I'll sleep tonight. We'll see what the day brings.

I met a couple of Swiss cyclists biking in the other direction, Fritz and his wife (whose name I could neither pronounce nor remember). They camped in a city park last night and enjoyed it, except that the sprinklers automatically went off at four in the morning. It's interesting that Montana small towns will let you camp in their city parks. Maybe I'll give that a try.

I talked to Sue, and I know that today she and Evan are having a good bike ride themselves. They're participating in the Scenic Shore 150, a ride from Milwaukee up to Door County that raises funds and awareness for the Leukemia and Lymphoma Society. Sue's mom died of complications from leukemia, and our family has participated in this event in her honor for the last ten years. I am enjoying my own ride, but I also wish I were riding with Evan and Sue. It's good to know that they're putting in some miles today too.

Having Evan and Kait participate in this event and ride the 150 miles, when they were kids, was significant. I didn't think much of it at the time, but going that far, at their age, was not typical. Their friends had bikes but never rode them outside of the neighborhood. To prepare for the Scenic Shore, our kids would go for rides up to fifty miles, often on their own. It was great sharing cycling with them; it's my hope that they ride bikes, lots of bikes, for their entire lives.

They started in a bike trailer, then graduated to a trail-a-bike, then to the back of a tandem, and eventually we got them each their own road bike. Now Kait keeps two of her own road bikes at college, and Evan plans to bring a mountain bike and a road bike with him when he goes to college next year. I'm glad this has become a part of their adult life.

I thought of Sue and Evan yesterday when I watched 35 cyclists going east to west on the road, all of them participating in the Bike the US for MS program. In 69 days, these riders will go from Maine to Washington State, a total of 4,295 miles. As a group, they raised $35,000 for MS research. I stopped and talked to a few of the riders; they were inspired to ride for a good cause.

Of course these rides—the Scenic Shore as well as Bike the US for MS—are fully supported. A van carries all your gear, so all you have to do is ride your road bike. I'm self-supported, with my 50 pounds of gear packed away in five bags attached to the bike. Riding a bike with a large group of people, fully supported, would be a great experience; it would be the opposite of what I'm experiencing now.

Today's ride is over. I ended up doing 125 miles. First day in the Great Plains, and I exceeded a century. I arrived in Havre at three in the afternoon; the wind was still blowing from the west at a good clip, so I opted to keep riding on to the town of Chinook. It's not big—only 1,200 inhabitants—but big enough to have a city park where I can throw up my tent.

When I first arrived at the park, I asked the manager of the public pool if this was the place where you could pitch a tent; it's my first experience camping in a public park, so I wasn't sure what I was doing. She said yes, I was in the right spot, and she showed me where to put up the tent, invited me to take a shower in the pool changing room, and offered to call her friend who runs the park to make sure they don't turn on the sprinklers in the middle of the night. In all, she was extremely helpful.

There are a lot of kids running around the park, because there's going to be a party at the community pool in about half an hour. They kept coming up to me when I was setting up the tent, asking questions like, "Do you live in there?" and "Is that your bike?" One girl asked where I was from, and I said Wisconsin. Then I tried to explain to her where Wisconsin is. I don't think she had heard of it before. They thought it was funny that I had a can of cold Dinty Moore Stew for dinner. I guess that is funny when you think about it.

It's good to see these kids running around the public park on a summer night. When I was their age, I too had free rein of the neighborhood. I tried to provide that same freedom for Kait and Evan when they were young, but it just wasn't part of the culture of suburban Milwaukee. All their friends had rigid schedules full of soccer games, piano lessons, dance recitals—it never ended. You couldn't go to a neighbor kid's house to see if he or she could play; you had to schedule a play date. This isn't news; it's become typical for suburban America. It's just good to see these kids living beyond the suburbs.

Before leaving the hotel this morning, I took the time to clean the bike. It was filthy, all the dirt I rode through in western Montana. It's good to look down and see a clean Salsa again. Tonight I'll do a thorough cleaning on the chain, rear cassette, cables—all the moving parts. I want to make sure Salsa makes it back to Milwaukee, and there's not a bike shop anywhere near this small town.

A final thought for the day. It was good to have the mountain passes to climb during the first week of this trip. The summits of the passes provided short-term goals, and the descents were the rewards. Now that I'm in the Plains, the wind is the mountain pass. If it's at your back, then you get the pleasure of coasting at twenty miles an hour. If it's a headwind, then you get the happiness of riding slowly. The difference is that one challenge is vertical and the other is horizontal. Today was horizontal, like every day for the rest of the ride. And it was a pleasure.

The mountains were also good, in that my legs feel strong. Ascending the five passes gave me the strength to go 125 miles today. We'll see how I feel in the morning.

DAY SIXTEEN

Last night was my third night alone, and I loved it. Meeting the people I've run into so far on this journey has been great. But it's also good to find time to be alone. After all, that was one of my reasons for going on this adventure: to create space for solitude.

I think it has to do with my desire to write. I love writing, although when I was growing up I was borderline illiterate. Throughout high school and my first year in college, I was placed in the remedial courses as a result of being diagnosed in tenth grade as a minor dyslexic. While my friends were in honors English classes talking about novels, I was in the remedial classroom, diagramming sentences.

Fortunately, during my junior year at Whitworth College, I took a course in American Literature from Dr. Lew Archer. I wrote an essay on religious symbolism in *The Adventures of Huckleberry Finn*; to my stark surprise, Lew responded to the ideas I presented in that essay with his own ideas. It was the first time anyone had acknowledged me as someone who could conjure up an original thought.

After that, everything changed. I took every course I could from Lew, simply because he included me in the discourse communities he engendered. I declared English as a major, took to creative writing with an emphasis in poetry, and fell in love with poets such as William Stafford and James Wright. They were voices that were male as well as sensitive and insightful, something I had never experienced before.

I graduated from Whitworth, and after a few years of working in a warehouse and backpacking around the world, I pursued a Masters of Fine Arts in Creative Writing with an emphasis in poetry at the University of Alaska, Fairbanks. The three years I spent there were rich in creative writing workshops and literature courses. I found my written voice, and I learned to appreciate the written voices of Pablo Neruda, Jane Hirschfield, Emily Dickinson, Jack Gilbert, Naomi Shahib Nye—a long and rich list.

And after Alaska I pursued a Ph.D. at Washington State University, while Sue pursued her veterinary degree, and got deep into rhetorical theory, Eastern philosophy, at-risk education, and qualitative research. I kept writing, and writing, and writing.

And it was wonderful. Not just because writing is an amazing experience when you commit to it on a daily basis, but because when you write you are typically alone. For an introvert, it's heaven. You don't have to say "I want to go be alone." You can simply say, "I'm going to go write," and people seem to be okay with that.

Even now, I'm sitting here clicking on the keyboard, and no one bothers me. No one asks what I'm doing. When I'm on the bike, they're curious about where I started and where I plan to end up. The laptop seems to be a privacy device. When you work the keyboard, people respect your space.

Of course, it could have something to do with the separation that technology creates. When I write, I'm head-down in my laptop. On the bike I'm looking up and forward, a physical position that enables facial contact and recognition.

It may also have something to do with cognitive focus. When I'm writing, I'm in "the zone." Even if a landmine exploded on the other end of this park, I might not look up. I tend to do this at home: Sue will ask me a question or ask that I do something with her, and I won't even hear what she said. She's the same way. We allow for it, because good work can come from such engagement in a task. But in social settings it can be an issue. Here in my tent in a city park in Montana, it's not an issue.

What I want to write about now is non-thought and the Great Plains. The two seem to be a match. Non-thought was a great vehicle for getting up those mountain passes in the Cascades and Rockies; instead of thinking about how much pain my legs were experiencing, I focused instead on the road itself, the bike, the breath in my body as it coincided with the circular motion of my legs clipped into the pedals. Breathe from the lower belly, pedal from the top of the legs—all part of the body's core. But in the Great Plains, it's different. The road stretches before you in a long straight line. What seems to change is the slight contour of the topography, the clouds slowly yet indefinitely shifting. There is a consistency to the Plains. In the mountains, every moment was new; every turn brought something different than before. Here, there is a constant in the landscape that enables the mind to lock into a sustained rhythm.

People ask me periodically how I can bike for eight to nine hours a day, day after day. I can't quickly or easily answer the question, because the answer is non-thought. It doesn't seem as if I'm in the saddle for daylong stretches; time becomes fluid. The mind is active but not exhausted with thought. I complete the day's ride, and the first thing I want to do is grab the laptop and write, because I want to capture the feeling I had during the course of the day, as well as the ideas that ran through my head.

Robert Pirsig, in *Zen and the Art of Motorcycle Maintenance*, writes about the "high country of the mind." He uses the high country as a metaphor for thought process, where those who think in abstraction often get lost wandering around:

> If all of human knowledge, everything that's known, is believed to be an enormous hierarchic structure, then the high country of the mind is found at the uppermost reaches of this structure in the most general, the most abstract considerations of all. Few people travel

here. There's no real profit to be made from wandering through it, yet like this high country of the material world all around us, it has its own austere beauty that to some people makes the hardships of traveling through it seem worthwhile.

I'm not the intellectual Pirsig is, and it hasn't been often that I've experienced the mental high country he describes. But right now, the Great Plains are my mental high country: a mental landscape, a mental road that goes on indefinitely, waiting to be traveled down. I'm getting to know this road. It's seeping into my head in such a way that I know this space will become the space of my dreams when the journey reaches completion.

Yesterday morning, when I was riding out of Shelby, I saw an animal cross the road in front of me. When I took a closer look at it as I passed, it looked like a wolf. I thought that couldn't be, a wolf in the wheat fields this far east of Glacier. But just now, I saw a coyote run across the road in front of me, and it was much smaller than the animal I saw yesterday.

Today is not yesterday: instead of a strong tailwind pushing me along, I'm bucking a headwind. The headwind of happiness. I'm averaging twelve miles an hour, reminding myself that the whole point is to go slow. Slow flow.

The headwind actually makes me pay much more attention to my form on the bike. I have to drop the shoulders, push the belly down so as to not use back muscles too much. I can't rely on the quads and hamstrings, but instead must constantly activate the core muscles. Toes pointed down, with little pressure on the feet. Breathing has to come from the lower part of the diaphragm—not only because this generates more oxygen flow, but also because breathing low connects to the top of the legs, thus giving a sense of connection between breathing motion and pedaling motion.

It isn't so much thinking about this physical process as it is getting into the habit of it. The more I do it, the less likely I won't do it. It just becomes a cycling style.

It's also the physical process for non-thought.

It's not as if this trip is one ongoing non-thought experience. Of course I'm thinking. But thought and non-thought are playing off each other. I focus on the breathing, the pedaling—and then an idea comes to mind. I pull the bike to the side of the road, lean it up against a mile marker, take out my laptop, lay it down on the back rack of the bike, fire it up, and write. I'll capture the idea, get back on the bike, do a few more miles, engage in non-thought, and then suddenly have another idea that makes me look for another place to pull the bike over and pull the laptop out of my rear pannier.

It's a fun way to write, writing on the side of the road. If I were riding with someone else, or with a group, it wouldn't be much fun for them. I'd have to tell them that I'll catch up, which I wouldn't want to do. Or they would have to wait for me, which they wouldn't want to do with my constant stopping. It's best this way, to ride and write on my own, in solitude.

An RV slowed to a stop in the middle of Highway 2, just before me. As I approached, the passenger side door opened, and a petite Japanese woman stepped out in front of my bike. She handed me a bottle of Aquafina and said, "You work so hard!" I had to agree, thank her for the bottle of water, and proceed to keep cycling, since there's not much shoulder on this two-lane highway.

I'm having lunch in Malta at a little sandwich shop that has Wi-Fi. I emailed my friends and family an update, a few stories from the last couple of days along with some photos. I've been trying to keep them apprised on my journey, but Wi-Fi is getting harder to find. When you enter a town you have to ask if they have it and, if so, where.

I checked the weather for this afternoon, and it doesn't look good. The temps are going to get up into the low nineties, and the south-by-southeast winds are going to pick up another mile per hour or two. I've logged 67 miles so far, and I have 41 to go. I'm going to have to top off all my water bottles to get through this stretch.

Earlier today, I nearly ran out of water. I carry three 24-ounce bottles, and I usually have more than enough to get from town to town. But I planned on refilling the bottles in Dodson, and Dodson ended up being a Montana ghost town. Two bars, both closed years ago. I was lucky that the RV stopped and the woman gave me that Aquafina.

The mosquitos have been bad today. All of a sudden, every time I'm near something green, there are forty mosquitos on my legs. I asked a Border Patrol agent in this sandwich shop what the deal is, and he said it's just a bad year for mosquitos. I asked if they're bad in Hinsdale, where I plan on camping tonight. All he said was, "Have some good bug spray."

I arrived at the Hinsdale Community Park, down by the Milk River. It was another big effort day: 115 miles. I'm not sure why I'm pushing myself so hard. Maybe it's the result of climbing the mountain passes, and I'm still attempting to match that effort.

I spoke with Sue on the phone. We're planning to meet in Northfield, Minnesota, so she and Evan can finish the ride with me from Minnesota to our home in Wisconsin. The best date for her to meet me in Northfield is August 6. That buys me plenty of time between now and then, so I don't have to push so hard if I don't want to. The question is whether I want to.

I love biking hard, but there should be limits. I could do another day of 100+ miles tomorrow, or I could dial it back to an 80-mile day and spend the night in Wolf Point. I don't know what I'll do; I'll make that decision tomorrow. But I think the decision will be telling.

Part of the reason I want to finish Montana is the shoulders of the roads. Most of the route takes you on Highway 2, and Highway 2 is infamous for its rumble-strips, those ridges they put into the shoulder so that if you're driving a car, and you drift onto the shoulder, the strip makes your suspension rumble to warn you to pay attention and pull back onto the road. It's great technology for drivers, but it ruins the road for cyclists. There are some stretches of highway that have double rumble-strips, which forces bicycle riders into the road, and that's not where you want to be when RVs and semis are coming up behind you. I've had to be smart about the strips, watching the mirror and keeping my ears attuned to the sound of upcoming traffic. It's easier with a tailwind, because the wind carries the sound of the vehicles to you. A headwind, on the other hand, makes it tricky.

This evening I checked the maps again, and the good news is that I have only another 40 miles to go on Highway 2. If I knock that out in the morning, the rumble-strip conundrum will be behind me.

It's been a great evening. After setting up camp, I walked to the bar in town and bought a couple of Pabst Blue Ribbons. I brought them back to camp and enjoyed them with a tin of Dinty Moore Beef Stew. That makes two evenings in a row with a cold can of Dinty Moore. Good stuff when you're on the road. After dinner, I took a swim in the Milk River. There were some local kids swimming too. Like the kids last night, they had a lot of questions about my trip. They think it's odd but cool that I would ride my bike so far for so long.

DAY SEVENTEEN

One in the morning, and I start to feel rain droplets through the mesh of the tent. I hadn't put up the rain fly the night before because the evening air was 90 degrees. I got up and crawled outside. There's a covered area in the park with a tin roof, for picnics I assume, so I threw the tent underneath it, along with the bike and panniers. Just in time. Now it's raining in sheets, and the sound of rain on the tin roof is deafening.

There are times in my life back in Milwaukee when I go through periods of melancholy. I wouldn't call it depression, just melancholy. I let Sue know when it's happening by referring to them as "Davy Days," which is a nice way of saying that I plan on spending some time alone until the mood dissipates. I take vitamin D daily and eat well. Wearing the color blue also seems to help. But what's interesting is that, since this trip began, I've had no feeling of melancholy whatsoever. I speculated that this might happen, given that a cross-country cyclist is outside the vast majority of the time, taking in copious quantities of sun, fresh air and, in this moment, the thick scent of rain on a parched landscape. I also feel deeply touched by the generosity of the people I've met.

I've done my research on melancholy. One definition would be "a feeling of pensive sadness, typically with no obvious cause." Pensive is defined as "engaged in, involving, or reflecting deep or serious thought." Depression, on the other hand is defined as "feelings of severe despondency and dejection." I wouldn't say that what

I experience is despondent or even breaches dejection; it's just a sadness that throws me into episodes of contemplation. I don't necessarily reflect on why I'm melancholic; rather, I enable the feeling to help me access ideas or concepts that overlap with the emotion. Eric G. Wilson, a leading expert in the relationship between literature and psychology, helps give it definition:

> There is a fine line between what I'm calling melancholia and what society calls depression. In my mind, what separates the two is degree of activity. Both forms are more or less chronic sadness that leads to ongoing unease with how things are — persistent feelings that the world as it is is not quite right, that it is a place of suffering, stupidity, and evil. Depression (as I see it, at least) causes apathy in the face of this unease, lethargy approaching total paralysis, an inability to feel much of anything one way or another. In contrast, melancholia (in my eyes) generates a deep feeling in regard to this same anxiety, a turbulence of heart that results in an active questioning of the status quo, a perpetual longing to create new ways of being and seeing.
>
> Our culture seems to confuse these two and thus treat melancholia as an aberrant state, a vile threat to our pervasive notions of happiness — happiness as immediate gratification, happiness as superficial comfort, happiness as static contentment.

I appreciate Wilson's definition because it connects melancholy to happiness. He sees our culture confusing happiness with gratification. I think we also confuse happiness with joy—an emotion that, like gratification, is short-lived. I am interested in a happiness that is deep-seated. Melancholy can overlap with happiness. Is it contradictory to say that? I don't think so. It's not just an issue of semantics. It's an issue of understanding what happiness is.

That's why Nishida's distinction between pleasure and happiness is so important to me. That's why I want to ride my bike through the afternoon heat for hundreds of miles. It makes me happy. This trip, the depth of happiness without a hint of melancholy, is rich.

The sound of trains in the distance. The sound of rain on this tin roof. Utter darkness. There's a poem in this moment.

Watching the sunrise as I enjoy another breakfast of peanut butter and jam on an English muffin with some Starbucks Via instant coffee. You would think I'd get tired of this meal. I doubt I'll have any of it once the trip ends.

Having an end date established has put my mind at ease. I have seventeen cycling days left. I'll need two days to get out of Montana, which leaves fifteen days between North Dakota and half of Minnesota. I can do that, with a few rest days thrown in.

Instead of busting out another day of 100+ miles, I'm going to dial it back to 80. I won't start until seven this morning; a bit of a late start is nice. And I won't have to ride through as much of the afternoon heat. Good decisions. After all, I don't want to be sick and tired of cycling by the time I get back to Milwaukee.

Every morning I repack my panniers, making sure everything is in its place. It's amazing how often I almost lose things. This morning, I found my cell phone lying beneath the picnic table in a thick pile of weeds. I must have dropped it there when I was eating dinner last night. It's a good thing I found the phone: it's my lifeline.

Last night I brought my laptop to the bar to do some wi-fi, and in my stupor from having biked too much yesterday, I left it there. The bartender ran me down and returned it to me. Mistakes like that are avoidable by hydrating more and biking a bit less. I can't afford to lose things, though it is interesting that what I nearly lost last night and this morning are electronics. You don't need the electronics to bike down the road.

But organizing your gear on the bike means you know where anything is at any moment. Here's my organizational schema, categorized by panniers:

Pannier	Gear
handlebar bag	• butt chamois • passport, credit cards, cash, other plastic cards (in a zipped compartment) • snack food (bananas, energy bars, etc.) • buff • tire pressure gauge • camera • phone • Chapstick • sunglasses • sun block • insect repellent • running hat
front left pannier	• whole food supplements • camp food • lighter • cooking gear (pans, cup, plates, utensils) • spices • toilet paper
front right pannier	• first aid kit • headlamp • camp food • stove and gas • bike lock

rear left pannier	• clothes:
	  • 3 shirts (Pearl Izumi brown, 2 Ironman shirts, yellow tri shirt)
	  • 2 pair biking shorts (road and mountain bike)
	  • gloves
	  • GoreTex shell
	  • pants
	  • 3 pair socks
	  • flip flops
	• computer
	• electronic cords (camera, phone, computer)

Pannier	Gear

rear left pannier	• bike parts:
	    • spare spokes
	    • chain bits and chain tool
	    • all-purpose tool
	    • allen wrenches
	    • bike cleaning supplies
	    • spare tubes
	    • chain lube and rag
	    • electric tape
	    • duct tape
	    • zip ties
	    • replacement parts for cycling shoes
	    • cassette / Freewheel Removal Tool
	    • tool for removing disk brakes

rear right pannier	• camp gear:
	    • tent stuff
	    • sleeping bag
	    • inflatable pillow
	• bathroom kit
	    • hand sanitizer
	    • toothpaste
	    • razor and shaving cream
	    • toothbrush
	    • deodorant
	    • ear cleaner
	    • bar of soap
	• camp towel
	• extra Ziploc and garbage bags
	• extra maps

other	• helmet • bungie cords • spare tire • dry bag that goes over back that holds sleeping roll, lounge chair, and tent poles • rearview mirror

It's 50 pounds of gear including the panniers. I've used everything. And so far, I'm toting the load just fine. When I look at this
list, I think about how there are things we need that are tangible.

Right now, that list meets my tangible needs. So much of what this trip is about is the need for the intangible.

I'm rolling down the road, keeping it to 14 miles per hour and enjoying the cool 62-degree morning air. Its 78 miles to Wolf Creek, my destination for this evening. A good decision. The hard work of cycling does make me happy. I'm reminded this morning that you have to balance happiness with pleasure. If you work to go to the top of the mountain pass, then you must enjoy the descent. I've spent years of my life climbing mountain passes without descending—just looking for the next mountain pass. Today is a blend: work on the bike, and arrive in Wolf Creek in time to look around a bit and have a beer.

I hope I remember all of this when the trip ends, when I'm back in Milwaukee living my daily life, riding my other bikes. The bicycling balance between happiness and pleasure. I have six bicycles, each one fulfilling a purpose:

- The touring bike: the Salsa, designed to carry cargo and go for hours on end

- The commuter: a Wabi, a single-speed steel-framed bike that is ideal for biking back and forth to work

- The road bike: a Trek Madone, made of carbon fiber and designed for long, fast weekend rides with Sue

- The mountain bike: a Trek Paragon, designed to maneuver down trails, over rocks and roots, through the trees of Wisconsin's southern Kettle Moraine State Forest

- The retro: a 1983 Trek 620, the bike I was riding on my 21st birthday when I was hit by the semi-truck, a bike that I recently refurbished back to its original glory

- The snow bike: an older Cannondale Super V, outfitted with studded tires and ready to roll through winter drifts

I try to ride every day, and every day brings different logistical needs. Having a variety of bikes helps meet those needs and keeps me on "the bike". When you look at all the bikes in the garage back home, it can appear excessive. But not to me. All I see is the potential for pleasure and happiness.

I stopped at a rest stop to refill my water bottles. I filled them at the campsite, but as I drank from them this morning, the water didn't taste quite right. Best to refill them with water from a tap instead of a campsite water pump near a river; drinking the wrong water could bring this trip to an end.

I also wanted to stop because I realized I haven't written about something I do frequently on this ride: I pray. Sometimes, the prayers are in full sentences—telling God, or the universe, just how grateful I am to be biking my way across the country and how thankful I am that I can be alone yet have someone at home who loves me. There's much to be grateful for, and it needs to be acknowledged.

The rest of the time, I pray non-verbally. This is my preferred method. It's simple, yet it does generally breach the culture's definition of what prayer is.

I was raised in a Christian family that had a strong relationship to our local Presbyterian church. It was common for me to attend church up to four times a week: Sunday morning service, Sunday evening service, Tuesday night for Boy Scouts (which was a religious experience in its own right), and Wednesday night mid-week service. That's a lot of time at church, and I learned to take it seriously. I also attended a private Christian junior high and high school, then went on to attend different church-affiliated colleges. My entire adolescent life was grounded in Christian faith communities. It was a good way to be raised. I had a loving family and extended faith community that provided a set of Bible-based morals that helped me make my way. Of course, it wasn't difficult to find my way through life, because all of my decisions, at least the big ones, were being made for me. I was fine with that, because I had a great deal of respect for those making the decisions.

That changed during my freshman year in college, when I decided to study New Testament Greek. I was considering a theology major so I could eventually establish a career in the church, probably as a missionary of some sort. Studying Greek was a challenge, but I had a good group of friends to study with, and the purpose driving it—to read Holy Scripture in its original format—was profound. It took the entire first year of study to get a handle on some of the passages in the Gospel According to Matthew, but I was getting the hang of it. What fascinated and frightened me was how different the original text was from the translations I'd been raised on. There was so much room for interpretation. In fact, there is no punctuation in Greek: it's up to the reader to determine where one sentence ends and the next begins, though the concept of "sentence" is also wildly different.

I was thrilled with this from an intellectual perspective, but emotionally it frightened me. I realized that my entire faith community and family made decisions based on a translation. I would often ask my Greek professor why certain passages in the New International Version, or the New American Standard Version, were translated a certain way, and he simply said that it was the prerogative of the translator. That didn't sit well with me, because I assumed that the translations I'd been raised on were the inspired, divine word of God. How could these words be divinely inspired, I wondered, if they were based in translation?

I wrestled with this question, and I brought it home with me during the summer break after my freshmen year. I asked my pastor how to reconcile it and, to my surprise, he was unwilling to engage in the conversation. That made me afraid of even talking about it, so I opted not to.

That was a mistake, because it made me afraid of my Greek class, so I dropped it. I didn't do well academically my sophomore year, so I transferred to another college to try to start over. That didn't work either, so my junior year I transferred again. On reflection, it's obvious that I was looking for a community that could help make sense of this conundrum. I enjoyed the experience of interpreting scripture in its original format, but no one in my faith community supported the act of interpretation.

That fall semester of my junior year, I took a course that changed my life. It was a course in Western Thought and Civilization, taught by Dr. Leonard Oakland at Whitworth College. In one of his lectures he talked about the epistemologies, or "ways of knowing," established by the Greeks. He said that they were broken into four categories:

- Authoritarianism: knowledge based on what our authorities tell us

- Empiricism: knowledge based on sensory intake

- Intuition: knowledge born from the mind (a priori as compared to a postiori)

- Innate: knowledge we are born with

Listening to his lecture, I realized that my entire life was based on authoritative knowledge. I didn't make big decisions on my own; they were made for me. Like many college students, the "way of knowing" I was beginning to become interested in was empiricism. In college there were many opportunities to be an empiricist, both inside and outside the classroom.

I kept taking English courses, and I learned how to consider alternative perspectives, how I should read supplementary text, how I was on the right track. Soon I started raising my hand in class, something I'd rarely done before, to contribute to the class discussion. And as the semesters rolled by, I began to develop the skills one needs to pursue a major in English. Which is what I did.

What does this have to do with a desire to engage in non-verbal prayer? What I learned from these experiences and people is that it's all up for interpretation. That's what I loved about majoring in English: you were expected to interpret the text. And that's why I went on to work in English departments in my masters and doctoral coursework.

So there it is. I'm an empiricist who embraces interpretation. That combination opens one up to any number of spiritual paradigms.

Because I received these ideas in a college classroom, rather than in a church, is probably why I am a college professor today.

I don't find language to be a good medium to communicate with the divine. It's a symbol system and, as Zen Master Dogen would suggest, a static symbol system cannot capture or express the dynamic nature of the divine. I do still often pray to God out loud in sentences, though, as I've been doing on this trip.

There is another point: I don't view nature as God's creation, but rather as God's manifestation. From my perspective, everything living is the divine. You are part of the divine, the apple I'm eating is part of the divine, I'm part of the divine—it's all God. That makes sense to me, so when I pray non-verbally, it's in line with Nishida's emphasis on non-thought. His pure experience theory. If I'm not thinking about my experience, then it's more likely I can simply be the experience. Less first person pronoun—less me, I, my. More emphasis on the Great Plains, the wind, the trees and streams I'm rolling past. If I'm awake and aware of these things, then I'm in a state of prayer.

For your typical Buddhist, that's rather basic. I don't consider myself a Buddhist, but I do like the way Eastern religions allow you to pick and choose from different faiths and different religious practices. Prayer, non-thought, pure experience, all get me to the same place.

I continue to develop my faith as I continue to pray to the divine. That's a big part of this trip: placing myself in landscape, in solitude, so I can pray.

Whoever designed Highway 2 east of Glasgow is not a cyclist. With 18 inches of shoulder, countless semi-trucks rushed by pulling farm equipment with signs reading OVERSIZED LOAD. Twice, when I saw that an oncoming vehicle was going to be beside a semi, right where I was going to be, I pulled off the road. Then, a funeral procession started to pass me. It was great that the long line of cars and pickup trucks were going slowly, but man, what a bad omen.

I made the mistake of focusing on the completion of the ride down Highway 2, thinking about that and nothing else, so that I neglected to see how far it was before I could get more water. I found out later that the temps in the afternoon reached 94 degrees, and I was burning up in the sun, rationing the water I had in hopes of making it to the next town where the map said there was a gas station. It turned out there was no gas station, just a tavern, so I went in with water bottles in hand to find four guys at the bar having a conversation. They all turned to look at me, an awkward moment, the four of them looking as if they'd been sitting there since the tavern opened and me waltzing in wearing bicycle gear. So I said, "Give me a PBR." The bartender served me a Pabst Blue Ribbon, and they laughed, calling me a union man. I had no idea what they were talking about, so I just drank my beer and listened to their conversation about a guy in town who had just had quadruple bypass surgery. The surgeons had a hard time finding stents in his legs because of his lifetime of smoking. "Smoking will get us all," they kept saying.

I filled up the water bottles and was heading down the road, when I realized that having a beer when I was dehydrated and pedaling against the afternoon sun had probably been a bad idea. It was an old empty highway, so it didn't matter much that I was weaving about the lane.

The Montana portion of this trip has been studded with cumulus clouds. As I made my way down the road, cloud shadows drifted onto my path and then drifted off. I pedaled as fast as I could to try to catch the ones before me, then slowed down when I reached their shade.

I'm staying in a private RV park that allows for tents. Fifteen dollars, and I can take a shower and throw my tent up on the lawn. I haven't showered or shaved in days.

Eating dinner on a picnic table in the center lawn, it dawns on me that no one else is outside. They're all in their fifth wheelers, doing whatever it is they do. Then I realize that, unlike me, everyone else lives here. It's not for those traveling down Highway 2. There are no other bike campers here this evening. I doubt this is a frequented spot on the Northern Tier.

DAY EIGHTEEN

Again, one in the morning. I'm not surprised to be awake. At home, I regularly wake in the middle of the night for hours at a time. I take pleasure in this time of night. I have the entire house to myself, except for the cats. Sometimes I'll sit on the front porch, looking up and down the empty street, enjoying the complete absence of humanity.

Here in Wolf Point an occasional car drives past on the highway, but that's it. No trains tonight, which is disappointing. I love the sound of trains. I enjoy writing this time of night. I ask my students what type of environment they create for themselves when it comes time to write. Some listen to music, others seek a quiet space in the library, some prefer writing in the company of their friends. But most have no method at all. The good writers do.

It opens a conversation in class about methodologies. I love finding the right way to get something done. Non-thought has served as a great method for me when it comes to distance bicycling as well as writing, but getting to that state requires a method. On this trip, I've had to adjust the method in order to simplify it. Really, on this journey all I have to do is eat, sleep, drink copious amounts of water, bike, and write. This simplification—not having to do a dozen other things that daily life requires—makes for an enjoyable writing process.

The pleasure I derive from cycling is directly connected to those moments when I get an idea that needs to be written down. I start looking for a safe place, where I can lean my bike up against a post, take out the laptop from the rear pannier, start it up, and write. Sometimes it takes a few miles to find that safe place on the shoulder of the road, and another idea will come to mind. Then another. I can juggle about three ideas in my head and remember them, but four is a stretch. When I'm able to put the ideas into words, there's a sensation of relief. At that point, getting back on the bike, I'm able to go back to non-thought.

Having so much time and space to bike, think and write: I can see how it could be addictive. It's good to know that this journey has an endpoint. That endpoint is what makes me appreciate moments like this, sitting in a one-person tent, on a Therm-a-Rest lounge chair, looking up at the stars through the tent's mesh, writing in the near-complete silence of the night.

At this point I'm doing 80 to 125 miles a day. Most of the other cycle tourers I meet are doing between 50 and 60 a day. I've been wondering why I'm doubling up the mileage. I think at first it was because I wanted to get back to see Sue. But now I realize that I'm pushing myself because I can. There have been aspects of my life over the last twenty years where I've had to dial it back, to compromise in order to meet my needs as well as the needs of others. Training for six Ironman events was fun, because you could spend an entire day going all out. What I'm experiencing now, going for big miles, is like what I wanted from Ironman. But Ironman was something I experienced while still engaged in day-to-day domestic existence. Fitting workouts in between the events of a daily routine. This bike trip is different. This is all in. I can go hard, and keep going, because I can.

I like to push, to find out what's possible. I hope that doesn't sound arrogant. There's the challenge you put before yourself, and there is yourself. Finishing this ride and doing it strong is a goal.

I hope to reach it, reflect, and take that knowledge into whatever comes next.

I pulled over on the side of the road and took out my laptop to capture an idea, and a van pulled up behind me. A guy got out and asked, "You want to fill up your water bottles?" I said, "You bet!" and went over to introduce myself. His name is Michael, and he's driving a support van for the Decatur Bicycle Club, five cyclists biking from Glacier National Park back to Illinois. He also invited me to join them at Horse Creek Campground in Circle. He said dinner is involved; I won't say no to that.

Circle is only nineteen miles ahead, so that would make today only a 55-miler. The temps could hit 98 degrees this afternoon. Maybe it's a good thing Michael offered me water and company, if for no other reason than to get me off the road.

Fast forward three hours, and I'm sitting in the Circle Library, taking in the marvelous splendor of air conditioning. I have to learn a lesson: don't drink beer when you're dehydrated. The first thing I did when I pulled into town was find the RV Park and campground. After setting up my tent in the shade of the only tree in the entire campground, I went to a gas station where they have five-dollar showers. Getting cleaned up was a great way to refresh. But at gas stations they sell beer, and I succumbed to a 24-ounce temptation, drinking it at the RV Park, in the shade of the tree near where I pitched my tent. Now, at the library, I'm trying my best to stay awake. I did fall asleep for a couple of hours. It was odd to wake up and see everyone doing just what they had been doing before I slept.

It's good to be indoors. I'm surfing the Internet, visiting my favorite websites, as if I were back at home. It's as if nothing had changed in the last two weeks. The stories are different, but the message is pretty much the same. The Republicans have too many presidential candidates, and the Democrats don't have enough.

Taylor Swift is not your friend. What young hipsters think of old hipsters. I wonder if I'll return to the surfing habit after this trip. At the moment, not even ESPN can hold my attention.

Accuweather.com does have some interesting information: the forecast for tomorrow is a high of 81 degrees, with 12-mile-per-hour winds from the northwest. That means a tailwind to North Dakota. If the prediction is correct, I could easily do the 111 miles it takes to get from here to Medora, where Theodore Roosevelt National Park is located. And that means a rest day.

I'm sweating in the tent. According to the Circle Bank reader board, today hit 100 degrees. I'm glad my ride ended at noon. The time in the library was restful. Hopefully, the air will start to cool down now that it's evening. I have to leave the rain fly on because of a chance of early morning thunderstorms. It may keep the rain out, but it also keeps the heat in. I doubt the weather channel has much luck predicting weather in Montana.

Today on the bike, I was thinking about something I teach my composition students: the "communication loop." It's a concept I thought up in graduate school, based on a similar paradigm created by Carl Jung. It looks like this:

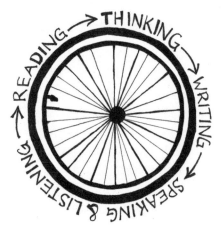

It spins like the wheel of a bicycle (of course). The idea is that, if you understand how you write, then it's more likely that you will learn something about how you read, speak, listen, and think. The wheel spins around, and all the spokes interconnect and propel the bicycle (or the self) forward. One impacts the other, and it all keeps spinning around.

When I tell my students this, they look somewhat surprised. After all, they've been taught how to read and write since early elementary school. If they're lucky, someone along the way taught them public speaking skills. But it's unlikely any of them have been taught how to listen, and none of them have been taught how to think.

I break it down for them into two categories:

- Communication with others: writing, speaking, listening
- Communication with self: writing, reading, thinking

Writing can fit into either category, depending on whether you're communicating with yourself (such as a journal) or with others (such as an essay for publication). Speaking and listening are social skills. Reading is typically for information acquisition—whether for entertainment, education, or inspiration.

Thinking is a category that the students are woefully unprepared to discuss. It's ironic, considering that one of the university's objectives is to teach students critical thinking skills, yet few faculty understand how thought process works. We tell students that they will become subject-matter experts in their given fields, but we don't tell them how the brain retains data. I argue that—often, to my freshmen—to understand how one thinks helps one understand how to write. And if the course objective is to learn how to write better, then we should also learn how we think and how to learn to think better.

I ask them how they believe that they think, what is happening up there during that time, and typically they have no response. I ask if they think in complete sentences, and they tell me that they don't know. I suggest that, if they think in complete sentences, it is more likely they will articulate sentences better when speaking to others; I also argue that thinking in complete sentences helps one communicate with one's self. I ask what they think about when they're writing an essay, and they begin to give me some information to work with. But the thought process they describe is similar to a five-paragraph essay, which they all typically learn how to write in high school English classes. Much of the work I do, especially at a school of engineering, is to get them to sustain a thought for more than a single paragraph.

The university I teach at boasts a 96 percent placement rate; our graduates average $57,000 per year starting salary. They are in high demand—the country needs engineers. But my students, most of them introverted, aren't studying so they can learn how to read and write, let alone think. A high percentage of them expect their post-secondary education to mirror a technical school rather than a university. I'm all about them learning technical content; engineers need to know their given disciplines. But they also need to know how to think creatively, how to come up with ideas, how to examine a problem, and how to communicate ideas effectively to a variety of audiences. These "soft skills" takes years, if not a lifetime, to engender. Life-long learning: you have to learn how to learn during your university years, so you can continue that process indefinitely.

If we teach students to write in terms of introduction, body, conclusion, then they should learn to speak this way as well—and we do that in speech courses. If they are reading, they should come to expect the same pattern. But do they think in terms of this same sequence?

My thought process is non-linear, unless I need to solve a problem through a logical sequence of steps. If that's the case, then I'll invoke logic to solve a given problem. Writing plays into this process by documenting the ideas. This often takes the form of an essay, but sometimes it looks like flow charts, bulleted lists, Venn diagrams, bubble graphs, and so on. It really depends on the nature of what you're thinking about: what type of pre-writing tool, or thought tool, you use to document the process.

But reflective thought, thinking without the writing—that's something we have to discuss in class and practice. I'll actually have them find a window in the building to stare out of, just so they can pay attention not only to what they think about but to how that happens and what it feels like. I'll take them to the museum on campus and do the same thing: sit in front of a painting and pay attention to what it does to your brain. They come back excited to talk about what happened, as if they had found a toy in the toy box that's always been there but which they've never played with. We'll return to the writing process, often with a completely new perspective. Not only are they learning how to write, but they're learning how to think in order to write. What are they thinking about before the essay? While generating the essay? How is editing the essay a different thought process? Just getting them to pay attention to their cognition helps them understand that writing isn't about fulfilling an assignment: it's about having an idea that's worth sharing, then sharing it in such a way that you can mass-distribute the information.

For this to happen a lot of unlearning has to take place, which is difficult because unlearning is harder than learning. They have to get past the five-paragraph essay. We have to read good essays, often written by fellow students, and ask questions about the relationship between the essay's form and its content. It goes on and on like this, all the while trying to get them to pay attention to what their brain is doing.

And when the course comes to completion, I tell them that they'll be writing for the rest of their lives, so please continue to engender this skill. And, obviously, they will be thinking for the rest of their lives, and how they think will morph as they develop as intellectual human beings. How will they think differently when they're no longer freshmen but seniors? I ask them to pay attention to this.

DAY NINETEEN

It's almost 7:00 a.m. I've been on the bike for an hour and a half, going slow. It's a ten-mile-per-hour pace. I was going this fast up the Washington mountain passes. I know I can go faster, but the body says ten miles per hour. Thank goodness I have a "slow" moral to turn to in moments like this. I have 110 miles to go today, and it will take me about eleven hours in the saddle to get it done.

One thing I learned from listening to The Sprocket Podcast, a podcast that focuses on "simplifying the good life," is that you lose your peripheral vision at about 15 miles per hour. So, if I want to maximize what I see, and if I want to focus on what is not directly in front of me, that drama on the side of the road, I'd best keep it slow and steady.

Had a great time last night with the Decatur Bicycle Club. Most of the members are in their seventies. The group has great cycling stamina. They do numerous group rides during the year, and one big ride like this one. We sat in the shade of an RV parked at the campground; they gave me a couple of bottles of Moose Drool Brown Ale, which happens to be one of my top three favorite beers. They also shared their dinner with me: sauerkraut with kielbasa sausage, a Mexican rice dish, and salad. The food was almost as good as the company. It wasn't that we had a great discussion; the day's ride zapped us all. It was just good to eat with people. I've enjoyed my time alone the past couple of days, but to commune you need a community.

I had a great morning phone conversation with Sue. We agreed that we'll meet in La Crosse, Wisconsin instead of Northfield, Minnesota, which is 128 miles further. This will make my last four days easier: I will only have to do 50 miles per day, all on bike path. Evan will drive Sue to La Crosse and take most of my gear back with him; Sue and I will credit card camp. These are good decisions. It's good to talk with Sue about sharing the end of the journey.

NORTH DAKOTA

DAY TWENTY

Yesterday, I pulled off 115 miles. That makes three days when I've done at least a century. It's fun to ride that much on a single day; I just need to make sure I don't do it on consecutive days. That can wipe me out.

Even though today is a rest day, I rode 36 miles through Theodore Roosevelt National Park. Instead of calling it a rest day, I'll refer to it as a pleasure day. Without the panniers and 50 pounds of gear, the Salsa hummed up and down the twisting road of the park's southern loop.

There are over three hundred bison in the park, and based on the freshness of the droppings on the pavement, I had to be careful not to descend on the downhills too quickly, in case I came upon a bison in the middle of the next turn. At one point there was a back-up of cars due to a bison in the road. The car at the front of the line tried passing him rather than letting him meander off. The bison let him know he was too close by rubbing up against his car and taking out the tail light. I decided to exercise my patience and made sure the last car in the line was between me and the bison.

What amazing animals. It's difficult to read the history of bison and the devastation that Americans brought upon them. There is a great deal of history that I'm learning about just by talking to people and reading roadside historical markers.

Because today is a pleasure day, I treated myself to breakfast: chicken fried steak in gravy, two eggs over easy, hash browns, wheat toast, and a bottomless mug of coffee. The waitress kept looking at me, probably because I was eating so quickly. Cycling makes you hungry. For lunch, I'm enjoying some Premium Midwestern Hickory Smoked Elk Summer Sausage and a Moose Drool.

I'm currently in the campground laundromat. I just took a cold shower for about half an hour, and I can't believe how clean I feel. There's complimentary coffee, so I'm set to sit inside this air-conditioned building for a while and think about the concept of teaching students how to think. When I teach composition I'm typically teaching first-year students, because it's a one-hundred level class. I don't push meta-cognition on them very hard, because the objective of the course is to help them learn how to write, so teaching them how they think serves the primary purpose of teaching them how to write.

When I teach a course in Creative Thinking, I'm teaching seniors. The course description reads as follows:

> The subject seeks a deeper understanding of the creative process by examining the nature of creativity and various competing and complimentary theories which seek to explain the nature of creativity and its origins. The course provides instruction beyond the scientific method and traditional problem solving, aiming for greater fluency in generating ideas, increased sensitivity to problems, greater intellectual flexibility, and the gaining of a broader range of new insights through an enhanced "openness to experience."

The first time I taught the class, the students were nonplussed. The course itself had a bad reputation on campus because the students didn't understand how the skills they would learn in it would transfer to their engineering courses. Or their careers. I had to figure out how to get their attention so they could build a bridge between creative thought process and their major engineering courses.

I learned to get my students' attention by saying things like, "If you want to make a five-figure salary, then learn how to solve other people's problems. But if you want to make a six-figure salary, be the employee that defines the problem—and then solves it." They like that message for two reasons: first, they want to make good money, and second, they want to dictate what work they do.

I'll ask them, "How many of you like to be told what to do?" They all agree that none of them like being told what to do. They are typically in the final quarter of their senior year of undergraduate college: they have been told what to do, and how to think, for the last four years. I tell them that I won't tell them what to do and that I'll give them assignments that are impossible to cheat on, because each is unique. There is no possible way to cheat, or plagiarize, or take credit for someone else's intellectual capital.

I do this by assigning an epiphany project. Basically, they have to have an epiphany, or a "realization of scale," during the course of a twelve-week quarter. They do not believe me when I hand out the assignment, because they generally believe that other people have epiphanies, and that epiphanies happen by accident.

Which is why I have them read William Duggan's *Strategic Intuition: The Creative Spark in Human Achievement*. In its first three chapters, the book basically outlines a method for having realizations of scale. Duggan introduces the concept of Strategic Intuition in the first several pages, telling his reader that Strategic Intuition is not like ordinary intuition. It's not emotional: it's cognitive. It's that flash of insight that cuts through the fog of your mind; it's when you're trying to solve a problem, and all the data is in your head, but you cannot connect the pieces. The epiphany is when those disparate pieces connect.

More importantly, Duggan asserts that the Strategic Intuition process is slow: "Strategic intuition is always slow, and it works for new situations, which is when you need your best idea.… You can't rush it." I tell my students that small problems require quick thought, and big problems require slow thought. The problem is that they don't know what slow thought is.

They understand quick thought; they engage in that way of

thinking all the time. Most of them take four or five classes each quarter and are working on multiple assignments. They cram for quizzes. They finish an assignment and move on to the next assignment, not seeing the need to transfer knowledge from one assignment to the other, since the overall curriculum is not designed to do this.

When I give them the Epiphany Project assignment, I tell them that it comes in three parts:

1. The first part takes place during the first week of the quarter, when each student defines a problem of scale that needs an epiphany in order to solve it.

2. The second part of the assignment unfolds during the course of the entire term: they are required to keep a "thought journal", to write down ideas that pertain to the problem they are trying to solve, so they can track the connection of smaller ideas in preparation for the "realization of scale."

3. The third and final part of the assignment is due at the final exam, when they present their epiphany (or why they did not have an epiphany) to the rest of the class. It's a scary assignment for these soon-to-graduate-and-enter-the-real-world seniors, because they have not, in their 16 years of education, been taught how to think slowly.

Once the first assignment is done, the students have to do research. They need the knowledge necessary to solve the problem. I recommend that they choose a problem that they already know something about; that way, they don't have to research new data and then engage in slow thought to solve it. Better to think slowly about a subject you're already familiar with.

Once they have the data, typically from a number of disciplines, we begin the exercise of slow thought. I'll have them find a window, sit in front of it, and engage in non-thought. To explain non-thought to them, I do a quick review of Nishida's Pure Experience theory and cross-pollinate it with Duggan's Strategic Intuition theory.

This process models the very interdisciplinarity that Duggan suggests is at the heart of epiphany. I don't ask my students to create new information—that's too difficult. I ask them to find information in one discipline and use it in another. For example, I had a student who loved to hunt with his father. But when the time came to pull the trigger, he would get "buck fever." In his first assignment, he wrote about how nervous he would get when it was his time to take the shot, because his father was there, and the pressure to get the shot was intense. He had a history of getting the shakes right before the shot, so he never bagged a buck. But it wasn't so much about not getting the buck as it was about disappointing his father.

His epiphany came in a conversation he was having with his girlfriend about her yoga class. He told her earlier about the problem he was going to solve with an epiphany, and how he didn't really believe he was capable of having an epiphany. They then talked about why his girlfriend seemed so relaxed all the time when he didn't, and that's when she told him that relaxation, for her, was in part the result of doing yoga.

The lightbulb went off in his head. He began reading up on yoga and breathing techniques. He started practicing yoga with his girlfriend in their apartment.

When it came time for his final exam presentation, he told his story. He thought yoga was not for him, but he was ready to try anything to get over buck fever. He learned how to breathe differently, and he practiced this breathing technique at the shooting range. He and his father went on a hunting trip to Wyoming over Thanksgiving break, and he bagged an antelope and a buck in one week, much to the pleasure of his father. He would breathe on a ten-point count, exhale, and pull the trigger. Yoga and hunting, two disciplines that came together for him to solve a larger problem: attaining the respect of his father.

I love the final exam in the Creative Thinking class, because stories like this stack up. A student solved the problem of being addicted to music by looking for music in non-musical mediums. A student who couldn't decide if he should start a job right after college or backpack through Europe with his girlfriend made a decision by reflecting on his $80,000 in student loans, which is a nice way of saying he started the job two days after graduation. Problems of scale being solved by undergraduate thinkers who practice slow, reflective thought. What I ask my students to do in the Creative Thinking class is what I'm doing on this big bike ride. I engage in non-thought, which slows my mind down as I'm physically biking at about 12 miles per hour for hours on end, and the mind does what it is designed to do. It connects various ideas that are in my short-term and long-term memory in such a way that new information presents itself. I pull the bike over to the side of the road, document the idea, and start to ride and think slowly again.

The question that I keep answering is, "What information presents itself?" That's what makes the blend of writing and riding so engaging. It's also interesting, when rereading some of these passages, to think about how the writing/riding process progresses as the trip unfolds. The thought process deepens as:

- The body gets in better physical condition, so that I think less about the body's ability to perform.
- The mind grows accustomed to the rhythm and duration of a day's riding.
- The knowledge gained from the act of bike touring minimizes the questions I have, the need for information, the unease of ignorance.

Bike touring is a discipline. Bike thinking is an interconnected extension of this discipline.

The problem with this discipline is that it will end when the trip ends. At home, I rarely go for a bike ride lasting more than two hours. I will miss biking, and engaging in slow-thought, eight to eleven hours a day.

The "idea" for this big bike ride came in the form of an epiphany. I was unhappy with my job as Dean of Students. I ran into a colleague by chance, and he told me about his summer bicycling adventures in northern Wisconsin. Later that week I went to the bike shop to get some work done on my road bike, and I happened to see the Salsa. And it clicked: I had to quit my job as Dean of Students and go back to my role as a member of the faculty because 1) I missed teaching, and 2) I wanted to spend my summers biking across the country. I wanted that bike. I wanted the tool necessary to have long, slow, deep, reflective thought as I peddled my way through the North American landscape.

Back at the campsite. It's good to have a rest day, because most of the time I'm biking, non-thinking, and thinking. Sitting around the campsite, drinking a few Moose Drools, is good. There's a good breeze from the south, and the sound of wind in these trees is rich. I listened to it all night last night.

I like this campground because, even though there are people staying here, it's quiet. In campgrounds, you can hear everything. And either you're aware that there are groups of people around you, or you aren't. When I spent the night in the private campground in the mountains west of Ione, Washington, I didn't know, when I arrived and registered for the site, that the campground bordered hundreds of miles of DNR roads used by dirt bikes and four wheelers. Before I was able to set up my tent in the campground, kids riding old two-stroke motorcycles were ripping their way through the area. That went on all night. I'm glad I had earplugs so I could sleep.

I don't mean to pass judgment on those who make loud sounds. It's just an observation: some campsites operate at full volume and others do not, and it's pretty much based on demographics. So far, I've stayed in bicycle-specific campsites, state campsites, federal park campsites, city parks, a private RV site: it's been a rich mix. But if I were to form a hypothesis based on the data gathered over the last three weeks, it would be this: the more machinery, the more noise.

That should seem obvious, but there's something profound in that realization. I like the bicycle because it makes hardly any noise. If Salsa does emit a rhythmical squeak or rub, I'll pull over and do a diagnosis to remedy the problem, because a sound coming from your bike is a problem. Yes, it's a mechanical issue: you don't want parts on the bike to wear unnecessarily because of unintended friction. But it's also an aesthetic issue. In those morning hours, when I've been in the mountains or in the plains, it's quiet. Still. The bicycle should not interrupt that.

I had no sense of this when crossing the country on a motorcycle or in a car. The silence, and the ability to hear yourself breathing, to hear and then watch the hawks and red-winged blackbirds fly beside you, is a big part of the draw to the bicycle.

DAY TWENTY-ONE

I'm sitting in the shade of a hay bale. It's still early, 7:00 a.m. In another thirty miles I change time zones again. I'll actually be on Wisconsin time.

I had a great phone call with Sue this morning. She's in Denver, about to give an eight-hour seminar to veterinarians on whole-food nutrition. We talked about how the nervousness she always gets before presenting has subsided, now that it's the day of the presentation. She also told me how she was chatting with the concierge at her hotel about the concierge's horse. Sue gave some suggestions regarding an illness the horse was having, and in return the concierge sent a bottle of wine up to Sue's room. That was a nice thing to do.

Sue and I speak by phone twice a day, morning and evening. It's good to stay in touch with her, to find out what's happening at home and how her work drama is unfolding. I tell her about the adventures I'm having and the people I'm meeting. If we keep doing this, it will make it easier to transition back into our daily life together.

I have a flip phone. I used to have a smart phone, but I had to give it up because I didn't like what it was doing to me. The biggest issue was that I was on it all the time, checking mail, texting, frequenting the weather app. Most of the time I was on it for no reason other than that I had nothing else to do.

When I received the smart phone, I knew I was getting something big. The ability to go online anytime, anywhere. Entertaining myself with the Comedy Central app so I could keep up on what my students thought was funny. Being able to communicate with Evan since he's a heavy text user. And that weather app. I gained a great deal, but in the back of my mind I knew I was giving something up, and what I gave up were those moments when there is nothing to do. The silent moments. Like walking from building to building on campus between classes. Before the smart phone, those moments would refresh my mind before entering the next classroom. With the smart phone, I was typically texting with students between classes, thus making it not separate one-hour classes, but one streaming two-hour teaching experience. And, as an introvert, it was wiping me out.

So I gave up the smart phone, and now I have a phone that serves only as a phone. Yes, you can text on it, but it takes forever to hit each key the correct number of times. I'm glad that Sue and I talk twice a day; and I'm glad we don't iChat. And I'm glad I'm emailing her and the rest of my family and friends a daily synopsis with a few photos attached, but I'm glad I'm not taking pictures with a phone and posting them on Facebook in real time. The non-real time aspect of the technology I'm choosing to use allows for a time lapse between when the photo is taken and when it's downloaded onto the laptop and then emailed once I find a wi-fi connection. That time lapse provides the opportunity to reflect on the bike as to which photos to share and how best to describe them. And that reflective thought helps the images make their way into my long-term memory. I want to be intentional about what I remember about this trip, and the photos I use to describe the experience are critical representations of the experience.

Similarly I like the quantity, and quality, of technology in the Salsa. I have a bag of tools, and I can fix a broken chain or a popped spoke. I can fix a flat and adjust the rear derailleur. When I used to tour by motorcycle, mechanical issues easily turned into a phone call to AAA. The hydraulics for the front disk break is leaking? Call AAA. The clutch burns up? Call AAA. A broken fuel line? AAA.

There are so many parts on a motorcycle that can go bad, and that's not the case with the bicycle. On the bicycle I am the engine, so if anything breaks that causes an issue, it's probably going to be me.

Now I'm at Mandy's Bagel Bar in Dickinson, enjoying a breakfast bagel with chive cream cheese and a tall coffee. The only creamer Mandy has is French Vanilla. It's interesting, a small detail like French Vanilla creamer, something I'd never use otherwise.

The idea of knowing something about maintenance, and knowing just how much technology to embrace so you can actually self-maintain what you use, extends into teaching students how to think well too. Thought is a powerful thing, but where do thoughts come from? Well, the mind. And how does one's mind actually work? And how does that working organism engender thought? I ask students to ask these questions, and I have to be prepared to answer them, even though I'm not a subject-matter expert on cognitive processes.

That's why I found an expert. His name is Terry Doyle, and he teaches at Ferris State University in Michigan. I heard Terry present several times at The Lilly North Conference on College and University Teaching and Learning. Each of the past four years he's given variations on the same topic, the new science of learning. In his presentations, he talks about how the brain works. Imagine you're a student, and your job is to learn, but no one teaches you how your brain works when you are learning. It's like sending a student into a garage to work on a car, handing him a set of complex tools, and telling him to fix the car but not teaching him how to use the tools.

Terry recently published a book, *The New Science of Learning: How to Learn in Harmony With Your Brain*. In it is a great passage on the neural network:

> Neuroscience researchers have shown that when you learn something new, there is a physical change in your brain. You have approximately 86 billion brain cells (Randerson, 2012), and when you learn something new, some of your brain cells establish connections with other brain cells to form new networks of cells, which

represent the new learning that has taken place. When frequently activated, these new networks have the potential to become long-term memories. In fact, every time you use or practice the newly learned information or fact, every time you use or practice the newly learned information or skill, the connections between the brain cells get stronger and recalling the information becomes easier. Establishing connections is like blazing a trail, which is a great deal of work. But every time the trail is used, it becomes more established and easier to follow.

I love telling students that learning is physical: that as you learn, you change your brain and leverage brain cells along a vast number of neural networks. It's not ethereal: it's physical. It's like bicycling: by climbing those mountain passes, my legs developed muscle that wasn't there, and my cardio strengthened, so that now that I'm in the Plains, I can consistently pump out a hundred miles a day.

Asking students to picture their neural network—connecting the short-term memory that resides in the frontal lobes to the long-term memory residing in the cerebellum—is critical. Having them physically touch their foreheads to symbolize short-term memory and the lower back of their heads to symbolize long-term memory drives it home.

Of course, this is an oversimplification of how the brain works, but at least it helps students understand that the brain isn't left-right. It's front to back. That dated concept of "left brain is technical and right brain is creative" is dangerous, because it gives my engineering students the opportunity to dismiss creative processes by simply saying "I'm left brained. I'm a technician." Talking about whole-brain, about front to back brain learning, opens the door to being both technical and creative, and that's the kind of learning I'm interested in teaching.

Terry also writes that the human brain is "constantly looking for new connections. Connections help you use prior knowledge to build bridges to new material, creating a more meaningful understanding of the new material." The brain doesn't just want to learn;

it learns. Whether we like it or not, we're processing about 60 bits per second, in terms of the input/output capacity during a specific task. So what are you going to learn today? And how is that information going to connect to what you've already learned? If you have a highly developed neural network in regard to that subject area, then the learning is easy. But if it's new data, and you have no background knowledge or experience in that area, then learning is difficult. That doesn't mean you can't learn it; you just have to build the network to get that information to your long-term memory.

I love riding my bike eight to ten hours a day, because it's teaching me something new about bicycling. I already knew quite a bit; ever since Marianne Harken taught me how to ride a bike back in second grade, I've been in love with cycling. To bike tour on this scale means I'm leveraging a network that gets the data straight into my long-term memory. And once it's there it's not going anywhere, as long as I use it on an ongoing basis.

I love riding my bike slowly, for the very reason that I want to remember as much of this ride as possible, to have the ride manifest itself in my mind, for the recall I hope to enact for the months, or years, I'll spend using the bike to commute or go on local excursions. In Milan Kundera's novella *Slowness*, he wrote that there is a secret bond between slowness and memory, between speed and forgetting:

> Consider this utterly commonplace situation: a man is walking down the street. At a certain moment, he tries to recall something, but the recollection escapes him. Automatically, he slows down. Meanwhile, a person who wants to forget a disagreeable incident he has just lived through starts unconsciously to speed up his pace, as if he were trying to distance himself from a thing still too close to him in time. In existential mathematics, that experience takes the form of two basic equations: the degree of slowness is directly proportional to the intensity of memory; the degree of speed is directly proportional to the intensity of forgetting.

If I want to live my life with great intentionality, to remember all the wonder and surprise I've experienced, then I need to move through life slowly. Slowness is a lifestyle, a way of living well. Our culture seems preoccupied with speed, with a constant flow of distraction and stimulation. I see it in my students.

I should teach at a university that offers a course in bicycling. The students could study the mechanics of the bike—they would take pleasure in that. But they should also have to study the relationship between the mechanics of the bike and the mechanics of the body. And, as an extension of the body's mechanisms, the mechanics of the mind.

I want my students to learn optimally, to understand that in order for the mind to work well, they have to maintain the body. Terry Doyle notes that the mind uses 25-30 percent of the body's energy every day, in the form of glucose. "This means that if you do not have a healthy, balanced diet and eat before you begin new learning," he writes, "you are starving your brain of the energy it needs to function properly, causing your brain to work much less efficiently." If a student comes to class eating a Pop Tart, I'll half-jokingly tell him that it may be tasty, but it's not good fuel for learning. And if he's going to pay $35,000 a year for his post-secondary education, he should think about coming to class prepared. That means doing your homework before class, eating well before class, getting enough sleep before class, working out before class—if you want the information to get to the long-term memory.

John Ratey, a professor of Psychiatry at Harvard Medical School, defines learning as information you still retain a year after you receive it. If you don't remember what you learned a year ago, then learning did not take place. When we talk about this in class, I have my students do an exercise: take out a piece of paper, and write down a list of information you learned last year. It's a great exercise, because so much of what they write down happens at college but not in the classroom. It helps guide the conversation about what learning is, if they want to learn in my class, and what exactly they want to retain. If we can get that far, then it's likely they will actually learn something.

My students are going to meet Terry Doyle. I talked to the Vice President of Academics, and he's going to invite him to my university during Orientation Week. All 650 of our incoming students will receive a copy of Terry's book and hear him present on learning. I made his book a required text for my freshman composition class, and I'll invite Terry to guest-lecture to the class. I want my students to know how their brains work, how to maintain it, and how to use it to learn.

Knowing how you think, becoming aware of your neural network, is a big step toward self-awareness. I'm a big fan of self-awareness. And the better I understand that I am an intelligent person who thinks well and has a method for learning, so I can self-manage the learning process, the more likely I will continue to be the person I am becoming. I want my students to share this information, because it's not just information. It's experience. It's neural science theory put into practice every time they enter the classroom. And the world is a classroom.

There's a book called *Solitude*, by Anthony Storre. To prepare for this big bike ride, I researched the topic of solitude. I didn't find a lot out there, which surprised me. There's a lot published on loneliness, but not much on solitude. Storre's book is rich in that it not only honors solitude, it talks about how it serves as a tool for self-discovery:

> The creative person is constantly seeking to discover himself, to remodel his own identity, finds this a valuable integrating process which, like meditation or prayer, has little to do with other people, but which has its own separate validity. His most significant moments are those in which he attains some new insight, or makes some new discovery; and these moments are chiefly, if not invariably, those in which he is alone.

Not all learning takes place in isolation, but for those of us who are introverted, solitude can be an important part of the learning process, depending on what you're trying to learn. Kait is learning to speak Mandarin, so she needs to learn with others just so she can experience dialogue in Chinese. Evan is learning how to perform in an orchestra, so although he practices his cello in the solitude of his bedroom, he learns how to be part of an orchestra when he is at school, performing with his classmates. What I'm learning right now is not social. I've been teaching Composition, Ethics, Creative Thinking, and Research Methods for over a decade, and the core concepts from these courses overlap. I've just never before had the opportunity to connect it all.

That's what's happening now, as I engage in non-thought, and then thought, rolling across the Great Plains in North Dakota.

A mile outside of Dickinson, I popped a spoke. It's ironic that earlier today I touted my expertise in minor bicycle mechanics. I do know how to replace a spoke. I've watched bike shop mechanics replace them several times, and I'm carrying all of the necessary equipment to do the job. I've just never done it before.

I zip-tied the broken spoke to one of the others. Salsa has disc brakes, so one broken spoke doesn't affect the handling per se.

Two days ago I sent an email to Father Odo, the monk who assists with guest stays at Assumption Abbey, a Benedictine abbey in Richardson, to see if I could stay there for a day. He's also the abbey's organist and has been serving there for 56 years. I read on a cyclist's blog that one can spend the night at the abbey, observe Vespers, and share meals. I was interested in Vespers and the ritual of praying five times a day, part of the practice of the Benedictine monks.

I rode the 26 miles to Assumption Abbey and was greeted by Father Odo. In the main office was a framed quotation:

Let all guests
Be received as
Christ.
Rule of Benedict, chapter 53

Father Odo showed me the room in the basement where I'd stay, a room with a shower, desk, and bed. We went to the cafeteria for some orange juice and cake and enjoyed our mutual introductions. He was curious about the bike ride, what I did for a living, and who waits for me back in Milwaukee. I asked about his way of life as a monk in North Dakota and learned that he entered the monkhood at the age of twenty.

When he went to help me move my bike and panniers to the room, I mentioned that I had broken a spoke. He said it's a problem he'd solved before on his bikes and wondered if he could give me a hand. For the next two hours, we fixed Salsa. We removed the wheel, the disc brake, the rear cassette, the tire tube and liner. The spoke broke inside the nipple, and I only had replacement spokes, not nipples, so Father Odo rooted around in the Abbey's storage room until he found a toolbox labeled "bicycle parts." Inside that box was a nipple that was a close match to the original and would work with the spare spoke. We put the spoke in, tightened it up, put the wheel back together, put the rim back on the bike to test its trueness, and it was fixed.

How Father Odo set the tension on the new spoke was fascinating. He plucked the other spokes, listening to their pitch, to get a sense of their tautness. He then tightened the new spoke, plucking it until its sound matched that of the other spokes. He's part bike mechanic, part musician.

What I enjoyed more than the actual bike repair process was the conversation I had with Father Odo while fixing the rim. I told him my preference for non-verbal prayer, and he agreed that non-verbal prayer is a good way to communicate with God. I also told him that

I do occasionally pray verbally but feel that spoken prayer is limited by the English language since language—the words and sentences we leverage to communicate—is a representation of reality, rather than reality itself. He acknowledged that limitation, but said that we use those tools God provides us. I asked what it's like to pray with his community of fellow monks five times every day. His response was rich not so much in what he said, but in the affection with which he described the ritual of communal prayer.

Benefiting from the generosity and assistance of others. It is the motif of this trip: when I need help, it offers itself.

After a shower and a nap, Father Odo came to my room and brought me to Vespers. The abbey is breathtaking. The woodwork and stained glass windows were hand-built over a hundred years ago in Milwaukee and transported to Richardson. Father Odo showed me where I would sit with the monks when we sing the prayers. I waited for the service to begin, taking in the incense and the soft candlelight.

The prayer service lasted less than half an hour. I've never experienced anything like it: a group of 35 men singing to God in hymns full of minor keys. It reminded me of the years I sang in my childhood church, but it differed in that, when growing up, I felt like an individual within a group of people. Tonight, I felt like a member of a group of men singing in unison to God.

The scripture reading came from the Gospel According to John: the story of Jesus breaking loaves and fishes to feed the five thousand. I had forgotten that, at the end of that passage, Jesus retreats to the mountains as a way of preventing the multitudes from declaring him their king. I can see why they would want to follow him, if he could perform miracles on their behalf. Yet he retreated to the mountains.

After Vespers, we went to the dining hall and enjoyed a meal of barbecue spare ribs, pasta salad, green beans fresh from the monks' garden, and moon pie. A feast for a touring cyclist. I thanked Father Odo for his hospitality and again thanked him for helping me with my bike. He graciously accepted my thanks, yet behaved as if this is what he does every day of his life.

DAY TWENTY-TWO

Six in the morning, and only a half hour into today's ride. Again I'm writing in the shadow of a hay bale. Love these hay bales on the shoulder of the road. The sun has crested the horizon, and the wind is from the southwest. It will help me today, because I hope to ride over a hundred miles: the fourth century of the trip. These long days are a challenge, and I'm learning that you do pay for that challenge the next day with aches you didn't know you could have. It makes you learn something new about yourself. I can do this. I am doing this.

As I left the abbey, I thought about faith. Not so much the faith that the monks have in the divine, but the faith that I have in the rear rim of Salsa. I think I've always had a misconstrued sense of what faith is, believing it's a magical force that enables what you want to happen to happen. What I have faith in at this moment is that Father Odo and I did a good job replacing a broken spoke, and that faith will prevent me from looking down at the rim every ten minutes, wondering when I'm going to hear the spoke pop, as maybe I would if I had repaired it myself. That wondering, or worrying, would take me out of the moment of the ride, away from non-thought and the ride itself. Faith can let the moment be the moment. Whether the rim fails is beyond my control. Father Odo and I did the best job we could do, given our shared knowledge and resources. And fixing the bike with him was a great experience.

That experience is feeding this one, so let me focus on the happiness derived from a functional rear rim. Have faith.

It reminds me of a conversation I had with Dr. Michael Myers, the faculty representative from the Philosophy Department who sat on my doctoral thesis committee. I was taking an independent study from him that focused on Nishida Kitaro's pure experience theory. I titled the final exam for the class "Losing Ego through Mu and Nishida." The essay focused on the concept of mu, a Zen Buddhist term for absolute nothingness: "By nothingness, mu does not infer the lack of existence, but rather a sense of reality which is 'paradoxically identical with the absolute'; mu does not distinguish any differentiation between individuals. Rather, the individual is determined by absolutely no-thing."

I wanted to write about mu in the final exam because Nishida uses it in reference to the religious aspect of pure experience, that sense of connecting to the divine through non-thought. I shared a story from my past religious experience: how losing ego through mu was far from my own previous religious journey. To illustrate the point, I also wrote about the moment I denied my faith in God on the shores of Whidbey Island, just twenty miles from where I started this big bike ride: I looked up to the sky and said, "God, I'm tired of pursuing you. It's time you pursued me." Then I walked over to my Harley Davidson Sportster, cracked the throttle, and sped down the road.

Dr. Myers gave positive feedback on the essay, with the exception of the section on my denial of faith. He asked that I describe that experience, so I told him. What Dr. Myers said in response has stuck with me for thirty years. "David," he said, "that wasn't a denial of faith. That was acceptance of faith." He declined to elaborate, leaving me to figure it out for myself.

I think I just figured it out. My moment of denial was in fact a moment of understanding. I changed the nature of my relationship with the divine because I was changing and, as a result, so was my understanding of God.

Maybe I'm just now able to connect the dots of my spiritual understanding because this expansive landscape is representative of my concept of God. For Nishida, God is what unites the self with nature: "God is not something that transcends reality, God is the basis of reality. God is that which dissolves the distinction between subjectivity and unites spirit and nature." God is what links us with nature because God did not create nature; rather, nature is a manifestation of God. To extinguish all thought of subjectivity and embrace nature is to embrace God.

A hundred miles of cycling in 94-degree heat.

I made it to the General Sibley Campground in Bismarck by three in the afternoon. I pulled up to the tent section of the park and saw a Surly Moonlander—a fine bike for off-road adventures—backed up next to a tent, so I rode up to find out who was inside. It was Adam, a cyclist from Maple Grove, Minnesota who is between jobs and just finished the Canadian portion of the Continental Divide Trail. He's also riding solo, so we had a lot to talk about: what it's like to bicycle tour alone, the head games associated with having only a few things to worry about, what type of gear to use when you're self-supported. It's a typical conversation when you meet another solo cyclist. He's been on the road for two months, but his trip has ended due to a bad rear rim. He's okay with it. He's already planning his next ride.

Next was a shower, followed by a bike ride into town to get more food. I was running low, so I made sure to get peanut butter, strawberry jam, English muffins, two apples, two bananas, a nectarine, eight energy bars, pasta salad from the deli, and a bottle of 14 Hands Hot to Trot Red Blend table wine. You can't buy a bottle of wine in a grocery store in North Dakota; it took some asking around to learn where the nearest liquor store was.

Now, back at camp, having enjoyed the pasta salad and half the bottle of 14 Hands, I'm thinking about Nishida. Not in a religious sense, but in relation to Sue. Nishida wrote an essay titled "Knowledge and Love," and although it was not originally included in his magnum opus *An Inquiry into the Good*, his translator, Abe Masao, opted to include it as the last chapter because it gave closure to the ideas in this philosophical treatise. In the essay, Nishida writes that "knowledge and love are the same mental activity; to know a thing we must love it, and to love a thing we must know it." For an academic this concept is significant, because academics are, or at least should be, in love with knowledge. To know something is to love it, and to love something is to know it. I tell my freshmen composition students that if they don't love writing—and most of them don't— then it's because they don't know it. They tend to agree, and we end up talking about what it would take for them to love the writing process. The same paradigm plays out for any subject I teach: If the student is not engaged in the subject, I ask if it's possible for him or her to love it.

What I love most in life is my wife. It gets back to that moral rule: "Love your wife, then your children, then everyone else." I love Sue most because, after twenty-five years of marriage, we know each other.

I've seen too many friends get divorced, then remarried, then divorced again. They never got to know the person they were married to. Or they never knew themselves in relation to that other person. At least that's the gist of the conversations I have with friends who need solace after having experienced the end of a long relationship.

I'm fortunate in that there is depth to Sue. I'm spending my lifetime getting to know her; there's much to know. For example, she never lets me repeat a story. If I told her a story ten years ago, she remembers it. If I tried retelling the same story to her now, she would tell me that I've already told her the story. You would think this would irritate me, but it doesn't. It actually makes me bring new information to our ongoing conversation on a consistent basis. I love that about her.

We've raised children together. We've helped each other navigate career changes. We've moved six times. She's navigated the loss of a parent. Did I mention that we raised children together?

Every morning, we take turns going through an established ritual. The alarm goes off at 5:30 a.m. If it's your turn, then you're the person who has to make coffee. You go downstairs to boil the water, then feed the dog, then feed the cats, then let the dog out in the back yard, then put the boiled water in the French press, then let the dog back in, then bring the coffee, dog and cats up to the bedroom, where the day begins with forty-five minutes of conversation. We do this every day, and every day the conversation is different. Sue is a wellspring of knowledge. That's one of the reasons I love her, and that's why I think of her when I think of Nishida's correlation between love and knowledge. The more I get to know Sue, the more I fall in love with her.

Here's a passage from Nishida's essay:

> When we are absorbed in something the self loves, for example, we are almost totally unconscious. We forget the self, and at this point an incomprehensible power beyond the self functions alone in all of its majesty; there is neither subject nor object, but only the true union of subject and object. Moreover, at this time knowledge in itself is love and love in itself is knowledge.

The state of total unconsciousness that Nishida identifies can happen when I'm with Sue, when I'm on a bike ride, when I'm absorbed in a good book. It happens when I'm engaged in what I know. That's what I love about being a generalist and not a specialist: there's a lot to love, because there's so much to know. Fixing the bike rim with Father Odo made me understand bike rims more, and that makes me love the bike more. Listening to Sue tell me about her kayaking adventure in the Rockies that happened this afternoon helps me love her more.

And I don't think we necessarily decide what it is we love. Joseph Campbell wrote that we should follow our bliss. I believe he's right, but I think the hard part, for most people, is to figure out what their bliss is. I've never had that problem.

The process of getting to know Sue was difficult, because we were in our early twenties, and I didn't want to share my entire self with someone else when I didn't yet know my entire self. I still don't know my entire self. That's one reason I'm a big fan of self-awareness: the more you know who you are, the more likely you can get to know someone else. Sue gave me time, decades, to get to know myself. And the more I understand who I am, the more I understand how I can love her.

Nishida writes that love is "the deepest knowledge of things. Analytical, inferential knowledge is a superficial knowledge, and it cannot grasp reality. We can reach reality only through love. Love is the culmination of knowledge." And Sue is my reality. I'm enjoying this adventure; I value the solitude. But I'm also acutely aware that I'll be with her again in ten days.

DAY TWENTY-THREE

Today is a test in non-thought. I am in the gas station in Hazelton, having a 12-inch chicken salad sub with all the veggies. The Coke that comes with it went fast. It's hot, already 90 degrees at 10:30 a.m., and I'm riding into a 20-mile-an-hour headwind. It's granny gear time again, very slow going.

The head games are in play. In Washington, I was blissfully distracted by the mountains. I had Logan Pass to look forward to, and after that Theodore Roosevelt National Park. Now I don't have any grand national park to look forward to. Knowing I'll see Sue in ten days makes me think about seeing Sue in ten days, and that doesn't help me bike into a headwind.

Here's another head game: When Sue and I talked on the phone this morning, she ended the call by telling me she had to go catch her flight from Denver back to Milwaukee—direct. She'll be home in time to wake Evan up. By then I won't even have made it to Napoleon, North Dakota. That thought just leads to other thoughts that involve Amtrak or Southwest Airlines, and those are not helpful thoughts when you're suffering. It's as if the suffering is there but the happiness is not.

Tomorrow's forecast is a high of 75 degrees with a strong wind from the west, a tailwind. I could drop some miles today in anticipation of to-morrow, assuming the forecast is accurate. That may be the smart thing to do, not that I have a history of choosing to do the smart thing.

Maybe the mind games are the result of my brain needing more liquid and nutrition to function. My brain is probably loving this Coke and sub.

So far, I'm passing the non-thought test. I don't think I'll get an A on it, just a passing grade. I'm 81 miles into today's ride, its 3:30 in the afternoon, and I have another 25 miles to go. Today will be another century. Trying to sit in the shade of a hay bale, but there's not much shade since the sun is high in the sky. Enjoying two bananas and some fig bars.

I could have ended the day ten miles back: the last town had camping in the city park. But I stopped just long enough to fill up my water bottles at the local bar, order a Coke, and get back on the bike. I like pushing myself, and today is a push. It was good to write about head games earlier today. Since then I've been aware of them, which has helped me focus on non-thought.

So much space. You can see for twenty miles in any direction. Not a single human. Just all this landscape. Part of me is ready to get back to regular life, but the rest of me is aware of the uniqueness of this situation. You couldn't ask for more solitude than I have right now.

So tired, and so full. The last 25 miles were brutal. I was riding due east all day, and all day there was a gale from the southeast. If happiness presented itself today in the form of wind, then I had a constant face-full of happiness. I kept it together until I was six miles from Gackle, the town where I planned to spend the night. I had to pull over in a driveway to assess how much water I had left: not much. Just then, a woman in a minivan pulled in the driveway and introduced herself as Brenda. She asked if I wanted some water, and I said, "Hell yes!" She went to her house and came back with four bottles of cold water. I drank two of them as we introduced ourselves to each other. She asked how far I'd ridden today, and when I told her I had started in Bismarck, she registered concern. "That's over a hundred miles," she said. She wanted to drive me into town in her pickup, but I declined the offer and thanked her. I was tempted, but I want to do this ride self-supported from start to end.

Things improved once I arrived in Gackle. Cycle tourers on the Northern Tier typically stay at The Honey Hub, a bicycle hostel run by Jason and Jennie Miller. Jason is a fifth-generation beekeeper and an avid cyclist who enjoys having bikers stay in a room at the back of their house. It's a sweet deal: access to a shower, laundry, wi-fi. After showering and starting the laundry, I walked into town, found Dani's Place, and ordered a beer and a pizza. I had no idea the pizza would be huge. I ate the entire thing.

While enjoying too much food, I started a conversation with Tom, a retired businessman who lives in Gackle. He asked about the trip. I mentioned that I was writing about the journey as it was taking place, and that a central theme in the writing is solitude. He then did what so many people have done on this trip: he opened up, telling me about how his wife died of cancer eight years ago, how he's afraid of being lonely, how he's learned to enjoy his own company. He misses his wife, but he said he's in a good place now.

Gackle seems to be a place where one has to embrace an inner sense of solitude. Fewer than 300 people live in this town riddled with empty buildings, surrounded by countless acres of rolling farmland.

DAY TWENTY-FOUR

One in the morning, and I'm listening to a thunderstorm. Rain pounds the patio outside the door of The Honey Hub's guestroom. Salsa's leaned up against the house, but I'm sure she's getting drenched. Yesterday I could have stopped in Hazelton and camped in the city park; it's a good thing I didn't make that decision. I love my one-person tent, and I appreciate how dry it's kept me on this trip. It's just nice, right now, to be in someone's home, sitting on a couch, watching lightning light up thunderheads through windows.

Somehow, I'm sunburned. I've been outside for over three weeks and have gone through eight ounces of Coppertone, yet my upper arms, which have already burned and peeled, are burned again. My back got burned, even though I had my reflective vest on all day. I don't think I completely understand just how hot it was yesterday. That 20-mile-an-hour wind from the southeast must have taken the bite off of the heat index.

It makes me wonder if yesterday was the hardest day of cycling I've ever endured. I've trained for a half-dozen Ironman events. I've done countless centuries. But none of those events or training rides were done on a heavy steel-frame touring bike with 50 pounds of gear strapped on, riding through a flat landscape that provided little windbreak.

Yet I enjoyed yesterday's ride. I mentioned earlier that I was glad to have written about mind games, because later in the day it helped bring awareness and thus prevent more mind games. In the same way, it's good I'm writing about non-thought and cycling: writing and reflecting about the act of non-thought, when I'm off the bike, is a great reinforcement for continuing to do it when I'm on the bike.

And it's not as if I knew how hard the ride was while I was doing it. Non-thought is not not thinking. Not thinking about the effect of the heat could have caused heat stroke. Such tragedies are acts of ignorance of what is happening in real time. Non-thought is quite the opposite. I knew I needed more electrolytes, so I took more electrolyte tablets. I knew I needed to fill the three water bottles and drink them as quickly as possible. I knew I needed to eat protein. And all of that happened yesterday, as I rode the 106 miles to Gackle. I don't mean to sound arrogant or pompous. I want to acknowledge that yesterday happened, that I'm feeling good right now in spite of the layered sunburn, and that I'm planning on riding to Kindred tomorrow even though it's, again, a hundred miles away.

Sue doesn't understand why I'm doing so much mileage. I'm not completely sure I do either, other than that I love to ride my bike and I enjoy testing myself to see just what I'm capable of doing. There have been times on this journey when I've felt the pain in my legs, and because I've felt that pain before during Ironman, I know how to react to it and adjust. Choosing to do what is difficult prepares you for difficulties.

Tadashi Ogawa wrote an essay on Nishida's philosophy and phenomenology. In it he claims that

> to the European way of thinking, Nishida thinks that one need not leave the realm of experience in order to construct a metaphysics. Vice versa, one can deepen experience. In willing, living and comprehending, we achieve it by means of experience…. Although pure experience is implicitly complicated, in the moment of perception it is always a simple fact.

Tadashi also wrote that Nishida lived his philosophy. Nishida wrote in his journal, "I am not a psychologist, nor a sociologist.

I am becoming a researcher of life." This is why I keep returning to Nishida when I'm trying to understand a profound experience. He bases metaphysics, how we interpret reality, in experience. I've read too many Western philosophers who write as if the purpose of philosophy is purely philosophical—not to help us experience life. Nishida is difficult to understand, but his core concept of pure experience, and its grounding in non-thought, helped me through yesterday's ride.

In my Ethics class, I talk to the students about metaphysics: How we each have a different way of viewing the world since we all come from different cultures and subcultures, have different families and faith communities, have been taught by different teachers. We each are different based on what we have learned in life: our authorities, our experiences, our intuitions and innate traits. We do in-class activities that help the students understand what their metaphysics are: what lens they use to interpret reality, what events colored that lens. I don't want them to see the world the way I see the world; I want them to understand how they see the world. With that knowledge, we're able to start a conversation about creating one's moral paradigm, establishing the rules that help us dictate our conduct or how we experience life.

Because one of my morals is "controlled risk," I was able to do something yesterday that involved a degree of risk. It's helpful that I've been in similar situations, and I look forward to future similar situations. But that's me, and that's how I want to experience life. I believe riding my bike through the wind and heat yesterday will make me a better ethics professor. I am making a sincere attempt to live my defined ethics. I want to do great things and have great experiences. It's hard, but the more you have such experiences, the less hard it is.

M. Scott Peck wrote: "Life is difficult…. Once we truly know that life is difficult—once we truly understand and accept it—then life is no longer difficult. Because once it is accepted, the fact that life is difficult no longer matters."

≈

Everything today was identical to yesterday, except for the wind's direction. It came strong from the west and, in eight hours, I rode the 105 miles to Kindred, where I'll camp in the city park. Salsa's average speed was 14 miles per hour with easy pedaling. Today, cycling was a pleasure.

Kindred is a wealthy farming town and, because it's a farming town, almost everyone who lives here is out farming. I arrived and checked out the city park, which is busy with kids playing in the city's outdoor pool. It's loud—the sound of kids playing in water—so I pedaled around town until I found Main Street: a post office, a diner, two bars. One bar doesn't open until four in the afternoon, so I went into the one that was open and met Theresa, the owner. She served me up the special and a Sam Adams. It's only two in the afternoon, and I have nowhere to go, so I'm going to hole up here for a while.

In all likelihood, today is the last day I'll do more than a hundred miles. It was fun doing high-mileage days crossing the Great Plains. But tomorrow I enter Minnesota, and the distance between here and La Crosse, where I will meet Sue in eight days, is 402 miles. That's an average of 50 miles a day for the rest of the trip. Any more high-mileage days would just get me to La Crosse too soon, and I'm not sure there's much in La Crosse for me other than waiting for Sue to arrive.

It could be good to slow the pace down toward the end of the trip. I've been working it pretty hard and enjoying it. I don't want to bring that energy with me when I reconnect with Sue. Right now I'm pretty focused. I'm either riding or writing. I need to pull out of this mental mode and get back to the thought process I had before the trip began, more open to interaction and dialogue. I've enjoyed the trip's thought process. It's been fabulous having hours on end for non-thought and cycling. But in the past I've made the mistake of leaving for periods of time and not transitioning back into domestic life. I don't want to make that mistake this time.

Eleven at night and I'm in the tent, unable to sleep because the wind hasn't subsided, and it's loud. The American flag blowing, the squeak of the flag pole swaying, the trees filled with bustling leaves. It's beautiful, this sound. I don't have the rain fly up, so I can see everything around me.

I also cannot sleep because I'm frustrated by the timing involved in this journey's completion. So far, each day, I've ridden Salsa as far as I've wanted to go. There have been no deadlines, no itinerary. But now I'm going to meet Sue on a specific date in a specific location, and I'm telling myself to dial back on the mileage so I don't get there too soon. Maybe instead I should tell myself to go ahead and have big rides if I feel like it. Do a few more hundred-mile days. And if I get to La Crosse a few days early, then that's okay. I can always take a rest day or two in La Crosse. It looks like they have a nice campground on the Mississippi River. How bad could that be?

Dinner tonight was fun. I made quinoa spaghetti in red sauce with shitake mushrooms and sliced summer sausage. It was fun because I purchased the spaghetti in Washington, the red sauce in Montana, and the dried mushrooms and summer sausage in North Dakota. I've been carrying that food around in my panniers for a long time. Not only was it a filling meal, but it will be good to lighten the load on the bike.

Just using the Optimus 99 was fun. I love that stove. I bought it when I was twenty years old, when I was a junior in college. I knew I wanted to do something big after graduation, but I wasn't sure if I should backpack through Europe or hike the Pacific Crest Trail. I had a sense that the decision would affect the rest of my life. In the hope that I'd hike the PCT, I started purchasing mountaineering gear: the Optimus, a Mountain Smith backpack (which Kait has since usurped and uses), an ice axe, good hiking boots. I love buying outdoor equipment. Of course, I didn't hike the PCT. I opted instead to backpack through Europe for five months. No regrets: it was an amazing experience that started my journey in global awareness. I just wonder sometimes how things would have been different had I made the other decision.

I bought some great items to get ready for this adventure: the tent I'm currently in, the sleeping bag I'm currently in, the Salsa and its panniers, cooking gear and bicycling equipment. Purchasing each piece over the course of the last year helped make this journey become real. After all, how could I not do this trip, if I invested so much financially and mentally in planning it?

In a way, maybe this big bike ride is my Pacific Crest Trail. Though on this journey, I stop in gas stations and grocery stores on a regular basis to get supplies. I'm on pavement. I meet a broad cross-section of people, not just other people doing what I'm doing. But maybe the next big bike ride will be in the Canadian Rockies, or possibly in the Sierra Nevadas. Maybe next time I'll get soft bags for my 29er mountain bike and hit the logging trails.

Maybe I feel the need to start dreaming about the next trip, and the gear I'll need for it, because I'm about to cross into Minnesota, and Minnesota is next to Wisconsin.

MINNESOTA

DAY TWENTY-FIVE

Almost five in the morning. I didn't sleep much last night because of the strong wind, but I wouldn't say I didn't sleep well. I woke throughout the night from dreams and listened to the wind, the sound of the flag.

The stars are still out. When this trip began, I'd wake every morning at this time and start taking the tent down and making breakfast so I could get on the road during those magical morning hours. Now that it's almost August, it's too dark to do that. The nights are longer, so the ride will have to wait another half hour. Besides, my destination is Pelican Rapids, Minnesota, only 65 miles from here. If I left now, with this westerly wind still blowing, I'd be there before noon, and that's too soon. Two days ago, I would have done anything for this wind. Now, if I used it to its capacity, I would do two days of riding in one, and I don't want to give up a day of riding for one big effort. Time to dial it back.

Dialing it back is on my mind. When the journey started, the problem I faced was solitude. I love being with Sue, and I love being alone. A nice problem to have, but a problem nonetheless. Now I've given myself a month of being alone for most each day, and I've loved it. Confirming my love of solitude doesn't solve the larger problem, though.

When I was in my early twenties, when Sue and I were just getting to know each other, I took the five-month trip to Europe and had an amazing experience. Every day my fellow travelers and

I would go in a new direction, to a new country, hitchhiking and Eurailing our way from place to place. Sue joined me on that trip for a week, and we had a great time. We started in Austria and ended in Rome, young and in love. It was one of the best weeks of my life, having both my girlfriend and my backpack in Europe.

The problem was when the trip ended. I flew home and was excited to see her, maybe too excited. I created an idea of who she was, an ideal, and that wasn't her. After a week or two of being back, the ideal Sue in my head didn't sync with the real Sue. There was also some ego involved, some self-absorption. I wasn't interested in returning to the details of domestic life. I wanted to travel, to be back on the road. As a result, I broke off our relationship. That lasted about three weeks. It took me that long to come to my senses, to realize that I couldn't be without her. I asked her to forgive me. It took some time; I had lost a great deal of her trust. But we did return to our relationship.

I went back to my job driving a furniture delivery truck, saved some money, and nine months later I traveled again. This time I went for three months to Asia: Hong Kong, China, Nepal, India, and Thailand. Again, an amazing experience, and again, I missed Sue terribly. And again, when I returned, I broke off our relationship. I couldn't have it both ways. I wanted to love her, but I also wanted to be free. So I moved to Fairbanks, Alaska, to start a master's degree in fine arts.

Four months went by before I came to my senses and realized that I couldn't be without her. On New Year's Eve, I called and asked if we could get back together again. But this time she smartened up. This time she told me I'd have to start to get some real help first. So I spent the next two years in counseling to figure out what was going on with my inability to stay in a committed relationship.

What I learned in those two years was mind-opening. I thought I'd talk with the therapist about my relationship with Sue, but I ended up spending most of our time talking about my relationship with my immediate family and, as a result, my fear of intimacy. There were a lot of unresolved issues that I wasn't aware of. There was also a great deal of ignorance: I still had to learn how to be in a committed relationship. I had to learn about compromise and how compromise is a good thing, because it enables you to support not only your own dreams but another's as well.

I also learned that it's okay to enjoy time alone. I am the youngest of four children. When I was a kid my parents were raising my older brother and sister, teenagers growing up in the seventies. Flower children. My parents had their hands full. And, back then, it was normal for a kid like me to eat breakfast, get on his bike, and not be home until dinner. I loved childhood. Like now, I would spend entire days riding my bike.

I'd also sit in a tree in a park in West Seattle, a mile from our house. It was a great tree to sit in because it had one branch that was perfectly flat; I could comfortably sit there, eat a lunch my mom had prepared for me, and watch people walk by. No one seemed to know or care that I was up there. The week before this trip started, I went back and visited that tree with the intention of climbing back up it and looking around for a while. Of course I couldn't; it's grown more than I have. The branch is now a good fifteen feet off the ground. The tree growing more than I have—that's a good metaphor.

When I was 24 years old, I learned that the desire to travel was in large part a desire to shirk commitment. Did I want to travel my whole life alone? No. I wanted to travel, but I wanted to live my life with Sue.

Six months later, Sue and I were engaged. She moved up to Alaska with me, and we shared a one-room cabin without running water. Talk about courage on her part: moving to Alaska's interior with her flaky fiancé who was studying the fine art of poetry.

Six months after that, we were married. That was twenty-five years ago. No regrets.

I'm reminded of those experiences because I am about to return to my commitments and responsibilities. It's good to recall what I learned from the therapist 26 years ago. My life isn't all about me.

I hope there will be another big bike ride next summer. It may not be this big, and I'll be okay with that. The relationship I have with Sue isn't going to be one where I hop on my bike and leave whenever I want. It took over a year to negotiate the generation of this trip; it should take at least another year to generate the next one.

And who knows, maybe Sue will want to get her own Salsa Vaya. Maybe the model up from mine with the Shimano 105 group. That would look good with some blue Ortlieb panniers.

In the next week, I want to prepare to re-enter my wonderful domestic life. I don't want to idealize it or Sue. I just want to get ready for returning to our sense of normal. Because, as amazing as this big bike ride has been, it's been far from the norm.

The stars are gone. It's still dark out, but a light shade of blue is on the horizon. It's time to start the stove and make some coffee.

On my wrist, I wear a Road ID with information that someone would need to see if something went wrong and I was incapacitated by the side of the road. Talk about controlled risk. Here's what my Road ID reads:

DAVE HOWELL

WHITEFISH BAY, WI USA

SUE (with phone number)

KAIT (with phone number)

BEE ALLERGY

HTFU

It's good data to have on your body, for three reasons:

1. The authorities or medics would know who to contact if I was unable to communicate.

2. There would be a distinct possibility that whatever went wrong was the result of a bee sting.

3. When I'm not happy and I'm suffering, sometimes I need to HTFU, to *harden the fuck up!* (Actually, I don't actively follow that moral anymore, but I did when I had the Road ID printed.)

I have a nice tan line beneath the Road ID. I take it off only when I sleep, and when I do take it off, I put it on Salsa.

I'm glad I have on my person the contact information of those who love me. I'm glad I have people to go home to.

In a coffee shop in Morehead, Minnesota, enjoying 16 ounces of drip and a yogurt parfait. There's a ton of muffins and cookies in the shop's display case, but I think I'm done with gluten for a while. A long while. I say that knowing how much pleasure comes from a good beer after a long day's ride. Maybe, when this trip ends, I'll finally transition from the gluten (beer) to the grape (wine). I've seen a lot of beer bellies on this trip. When the trip started, I saw one on me.

I knew I was approaching the Fargo/Morehead area this morning, because cars were passing each other. I don't think I've seen a car pass another car since Bismarck. On my way into town, I saw a Porsche 911. And everyone is on a cell phone. The cyclists I saw commuting to work were all wearing ear buds.

The weather forecast is outstanding, a strong wind from the west for the next five days, high temperatures in the low eighties.

I'm having a wonderful stay with my Warm Shower hosts, Gretchen and Andrew Johnson. They live in Pelican Rapids above their business, an ice cream and flower shop. They also rent kayaks, grow hops, and dabble in growing turkey eggs. They're fascinating people to talk to.

Gretchen let me into their apartment, showed me around, and

introduced me to their two cats. She had to return to the business, so she left me with the cats, who are very affectionate, rubbing me up with their cheeks as they purr. The apartment is in a state of remodel. They are fixing it up one room at a time, refurbishing the original wood floors, sanding and re-staining the ornamental trim that must be a hundred years old.

It was a good day's ride. The winds are steadily strong—either you're propelled forward when it's behind you, or you're struggling to hold your line when it's a side wind. It took a great deal of energy, both physical and mental, to ride in a straight line. The first thing I did when I arrived was to shower, then off to eat an early dinner at the Mexican restaurant in town, then a two-hour nap. I woke up in time to enjoy Gretchen and Andrew's good company— but man, I was gassed.

When I wasn't battling the wind today, I was thinking about how fortunate I am to be happily married. I don't know many couples who have been married as long as we have who are happy together. I think the secret to our marriage is that we talk. It sounds simple, but it's at the heart of what makes our relationship work. Robert Pirsig wrote that we are "in such a hurry most of the time we never get much chance to talk. The result is a kind of endless day-to-day shallowness, a monotony that leaves a person wondering years later where all the time went and sorry that it's all gone." On this big bike ride, I don't think I've had a shallow conversation yet. Maybe it's because people are asking about the trip, which is an open door to telling all kinds of interesting stories.

Being in a good relationship provides a great deal of peace of mind, and peace of mind is not easy to maintain. Here's another quote from Pirsig, one I care about enough to have had laminated and keep in my wallet, right next to my list of personal morals:

Peace of mind isn't at all superficial. ... It's the whole thing. That which produced it is good maintenance; that which disturbs it is poor maintenance. What we call workability of the machine is just an objectification of this peace of mind. The ultimate test's always your own serenity. If you don't have this when you start and maintain it while you're working you're likely to build your personal problems right into the machine itself.

Pirsig is using motorcycle maintenance as his metaphor for self-maintenance. The same can apply to marital maintenance. Does the marriage work? A lot depends on whether you have peace of mind, both as an individual and as a member of the relationship.

A steady and engaging dialogue with Sue is a big part of our maintenance. This evening, we had a great phone conversation. We didn't discuss anything extraordinary. We simply talked about how she and Evan went out for dinner at one of our favorite Korean restaurants in Milwaukee and found a secret rooftop Zen garden on top of the building. Then they were going to go to the local bike shop to pick up Sue's bike: she had wider tires put on it for the ride we'll be doing together from La Crosse back to Milwaukee, since much of the route is on crushed-shale trails. These are just details in her day, but she shares them with such enthusiasm that it becomes part of my day. She asks what happened to me, and I tell her about the strong winds on today's ride, about Gretchen and Andrew, how tired I was at the end of today's ride, how much I enjoyed taking a shower and nap. She's interested in what I have to say, and her narrative and mine are still intertwining even though we haven't seen each other in nearly a month. This type of dialogue takes regular practice and maintenance.

The summer before we were married, Sue and I saw a couples counselor named Joyce. Joyce made us think about things we hadn't yet thought about and told us things we needed to hear. One thing she told us was the three things that she saw ruin marriages:

1. Sex

2. Money

3. Basic communication

You have to be open about these three things. And, of the three, I think basic communication is the key. Sex and money are really subsets of basic communication.

Getting away from each other periodically is part of the maintenance as well. This big bike ride is an example of a personal vacation. It's good to have common interests and goals, but it's good to balance that with interests and goals that are your own, yet supported by your partner.

I don't mean this to sound like I'm giving marriage advice. I'm just trying to articulate why I am deeply happy. We work at our marriage, and that brings us happiness. You have to have peace of mind, and that's not going to happen if you're at odds with the person with whom you share your life.

I think it also helps that we're both introverted. We have a great deal invested in each other. We've put all our eggs in one basket. I'm okay with that.

DAY TWENTY-SIX

Seven in the morning, and I'm on the side of Highway 3 watching the sunrise. I've already enjoyed a great breakfast of farm-fresh eggs and coffee, thanks to the generosity of Gretchen and Andrew. It's nice when the night before they show me everything I need to know to make a nice breakfast at five in the morning, three hours before they get up. It still amazes me that people who participate in the Warm Showers program are so open to sharing their homes. I hope it always amazes me.

I had a great morning phone call with Sue. We talked about what I wrote yesterday, that communication is the key to a healthy marriage. I guess we were engaged in meta-communication, communicating about communicating.

After the call, I started the day's ride again and thought about something else that is key to the serenity of a relationship, and that's avoiding drama. Sue and I are Survivor fans; I love watching the television show because people have to figure out how to survive both the natural environment and each other. There was one season years ago that had a participant, Vecepia Towery, who did all she could to stay in the background. She would set up the other contestants, those who were doing whatever it took to establish themselves as leaders, by lavishing them with praise and telling them what great leaders they were. As a result, these dominant participants would overly assert themselves and as a result get voted off the island. Vecepia's big line was, "Too much drama." She went on to win the million dollars.

That stuck with me, because our culture is in love with drama. We all talk to each other about the drama of our lives. We're consumed by the drama of reality television shows. We're addicted to the sensational and the controversial.

The most dramatic thing that has happened so far on this trip was fixing a broken spoke with a monk. Well, that and running into a wolf and bear in the middle of nowhere.

If you minimize the drama and keep your life simple, then when life does present the dramatic, you're ready for it. You learn that you're about to lose your job because you're too good at it, or you walk outside the library to see your son get hit by a car, or you find out your mother has leukemia—these are some of the dramatic events that Sue has had to face over the past decade. She's weathered each storm, because she doesn't generate too much of her own drama.

It also helps that Sue was a theatre major as an undergraduate. This woman understands drama.

When I was an English major, my appreciation for the right kind of minimized drama was the result of Lew Archer's influence and his recognition of my metaphysic, but it was also an introduction to poetry, to the drama one finds in poetic solitude, the solace in slowed language. I was in the college bookstore buying textbooks—which is a great experience for English majors, because you're basically buying works of literature—and ran across *Stories that Could Be True*, the collected poems of William Stafford. Stafford was a poet from Oregon, and I was not only moved by the descriptions of landscape I was intimately familiar with, but more importantly by the lyrics of a mature, sensitive male voice. His poem, "Traveling through the Dark," cut deep into me. In the poem, the protagonist is driving down a canyon road at night and has to stop. A doe is dead on the side of the road, hit by the previous car. Inside the doe is its faun, still alive but never to be born:

> The car aimed ahead its lowered parking lights;
> under the hood purred the steady engine.
> I stood in the glare of the warm exhaust turning red;

around our group I could hear the wilderness listen.

I thought hard for us all—my only swerving—,
then pushed her over the edge into the river.

The voice of the poet is a reflective voice: "I thought hard for us all—my only swerving—." It's the voice of someone standing on the side of the road at night, alone but for the doe and her unborn fawn. The car is personified, looking down the road with its lowered parking lights. But it's just the poet. There is no second human being present for the poet to talk to about his decision to push the deer into the river. He has to make the decision on his own.

I came to appreciate the drama of poetry. You don't need two people interacting; that's the stuff of fiction and stage plays. You don't need dialogue, just an internal monologue. It's just the voice of the poet, the perspective of one.

This distinction has always made me want to read and write poetry. It's also why I think poetry as a genre is dying. The reading public is less interested in the interior landscape of the individual. If poetry sells, it's in the form of poetry slams, of rap, of human-to-human drama. Too much drama.

For some reason, I bonked coming into Fergus Falls. Only 20 miles into today's ride, and after having eaten three eggs at Gretchen's this morning. I combated the bonk with restaurant coffee, a breakfast sandwich, a hardboiled egg, and a slice of coffee cake.

It could be more of a cognitive bonk. Maybe my brain is calling out for a rest day.

The nice thing about leaving Fergus Falls is that the route leaves the roads and moves onto bike paths. About 80 miles of bike paths from here going all the way into the Twin Cities. No more checking the rearview mirror for harvest trucks and earth movers. No more rumble strips, broken glass, tar snakes and semi-truck tire shards. Just pavement designed for cyclists.

Sixty miles into the bike path, and all is good. Except for my butt. For some reason, my butt is killing me. I'm pedaling standing as much as I'm sitting. Going back and forth is easy enough once a rhythm is established.

Thank God for Minnesota's bike path system. It's fun to bike tour on the same paths that everyday riders are using. For the last four weeks, other bicycle riders had setups like mine, with panniers or bike trailers attached. Now there are folks riding comfort bikes going past me, just enjoying a short ride on a Thursday afternoon.

That is one big difference between Minnesota and the other states I've traveled through: recreation. Especially in east Montana and North Dakota, you don't see people just having fun. Right now, I'm sitting on a bench beside Lake Darling, in a park with a nice fire pit and benches and a dock that I was just sitting on so I could soak my feet in the water. On the other side of the lake is a boat pulling a water skier, accompanied by jet skis.

Gretchen, last night's Warm Showers host, had a scale in her kitchen. I decided to give the Northern Tier Weight Loss Program a test to see if it actually works, if you really do lose a pound a day riding fully supported across the country. It's close: in the last 25 days, I've lost 20 pounds. I'd probably be 25 for 25 if I hadn't been drinking so much beer on this trip, but that's something I can live with.

Before I turned 50, I reflected on what I'd like to do different in the next decade of my life, and I came up with one thing: lose weight. Not for the sake of vanity, but more so I could enjoy what I enjoy more, the bicycling and running. Now I'm a year into my fifties, and it turns out losing weight was the easy part: just ride your bike for a month straight. The hard part is going to be figuring out how to change my domestic life so my leaner self sticks around for the rest of the decade. Ten days until I'm home. Can I lose ten more pounds? I know that the leaner you get, the harder it is to lose weight. We'll see what happens when I step on the scale at home.

∂

Evening at an RV Park in Sauk Centre. I just mapped out where I'll be staying tomorrow night. The night after that is a bit of a mystery, but other than that the rest of the trip is planned in terms of lodging.

There was some melancholy today, so it was a good thing I was on my own. Between the tailwind and the bike path, it was a great day for bicycling. I think I'm mentally preparing for the end of the trip. I gave so much energy to get ready to start the trip, an entire year of planning and preparation. Most of the journey required real-time logistical processing, just to figure out what I was going to eat and where I was going to stay on any given day. Now that I'm in Minnesota, there are countless culinary options. Campgrounds abound. It's not as difficult as mapping out my way across the mountains or the Great Plains, and I think the eased challenge, the domesticity of Minnesota, makes it all less engaging.

I also gave a great deal of thought today to seeing Sue again. That doesn't help me stay in the now. I have to do a better job with nonthought between now and when I see Sue in six days.

DAY TWENTY-SEVEN

It's difficult to sleep in the RV park. Though it's one in the morning, people are still up socializing, having fun, letting their kids have fun. I have to remind myself that I'm the non-traditional traveler here, the guy on a bike in a tent. Everyone else seems to have a fifth wheeler to go in and out of.

I don't mean to pass judgment, but I got out of the tent to go to the restroom, and I saw a father show his son how to rack someone in the balls. At one in the morning.

You ride a bike, especially on a solo ride, and you're enveloped in silence. I can see how this sport draws those who are attracted to the sound of landscape, rather than bringing sound to the landscape.

It becomes obvious, when I think about it, that the cyclists I've met on this trip are a reflective bunch. They tell detailed, organized narratives, as if they've processed them in their heads over and over. They remember the minutiae of similar experiences. Like me, they're plodding along in the midst of landscape and thought.

If you have a fifth wheeler, it's a moot issue. I love this tent because the only thing between you and the environment is a thin mesh. That doesn't help me sleep this evening, though.

This big bike ride is taking a mental toll. Needing a boost, I went back through all the photographs I've taken on this journey. It was good medicine, to remember the amazing places I've ridden through, the great people I've met, the weird meals eaten. You can forget how tall the Rockies are or how vast the North Dakota plains appear; I'm glad these images are here to remind me of where I've been.

Yesterday I gave thought to the trip's end, and it compromised the day. The end will arrive; this trip is impermanent. I need to remember to enjoy the journey while it's taking place. I'll have the rest of the year to remember moments like this and plan for more.

Seven in the morning. I'm in a coffee shop enjoying a slice of spinach-Swiss quiche along with an Americano—and a shot of espresso on the side. Needless to say, I'm not in North Dakota. This bothered me yesterday, no longer being in the rustic West. Maybe I should just enjoy the quiche, appreciate the bike path for what it is designed to do—keep cyclists safe—and roll on home. Just because there are no mountains to climb or plains to cross doesn't mean today will be any less of an experience. It's just pleasant, and I have to remind myself that there's nothing wrong with a pleasant bike ride.

The real problem of yesterday was my ego. I was getting into a "me, I, my" mode. When is my trip going to end, when am I going to see my wife, how many more miles do I have to go before I can get off my bike? All that first-person pronoun can ruin your day, which is a waste when you're cycling through the Lake Wobegon district.

Nishida wrote a wonderful essay on "An Explanation of Beauty." It's a dense essay full of references to the Japanese word muga, or egolessness. To love someone or something completely is to extinguish the ego in the process of loving: "When we are absorbed in something the self loves, for example, we are almost totally unconscious. We forget the self, and at this point an incomprehensible power beyond the self functions alone in all of its majesty; there is neither subject nor object, but only the true union of subject and object." In the essay, he writes about intuitive truth that comes from within:

Occasionally people vainly esteem logical truth and reject intuitive truth as being the mere fancy of poets. However, in my opinion, this intuitive truth is attained when we have separated from the self and become one with things. In other words, it is a truth seen with the eyes of God. Since this kind of intuitive truth penetrates into the profound secrets of the universe, it is far deeper and greater than the logical truth obtained through ordinary thought and discrimination. Even if someday the time should come when scholars no longer pay any attention to the great philosophies of Kant and Hegel, will not the words of Goethe and Shakespeare continue to be transmitted for countless generations as mirrors of the human heart?

On this big bike ride I've been reflecting on poetry, on the nature of God, the "profound secrets of the universe," because it all seems to be connecting. There's enough time and space to connect a good William Stafford poem to the philosophy of Nishida Kitaro.

I wish my engineering students could take a course on "Reflective Thought and Bicycle Touring." That would be a fun class to teach. We'd hold class in the morning, introduce some concepts, and let them go off on their bikes, to embrace the ride while reflecting on the content of the class. Then we'd get together at the end of the ride, over dinner at some city park campground, and discuss what they thought about and experienced over eight or nine hours of cycling.

I should offer this class as a summer course because, like Nishida, I worry that my students won't pay any attention to Kant and Hegel, but also that they won't know the words of Goethe and Shakespeare. That's why the job of teaching matters. We have to bring these philosophers and poets into the presence of students. And then we have to create an opportunity to reflect and process those big-picture concepts. Hence big bike rides.

Today is the day of the "pure bicycling experience," henceforth to be known as "PBE." They recently paved the Lake Wobegon Bike Trail, so the pedaling is pleasurable. A light tailwind continues to serve as a welcome companion.

I have to do some research to find out if Nishida, or any of my other favorite philosophers and poets, bicycled.

It's 10:30 in the morning, and I've already bonked. Not a cognitive bonk—a straight-out loss of energy from head to toe. I stopped on the trail and ate bananas and dried fruit, but the body was asking for more. Rolling through Holdingford, I saw a sign for the Lake Wobegon Trailside Café. I pulled into town, parked Salsa in front of the café, met the waitress, and ordered the breakfast burrito: three eggs, cheddar, onions, mushrooms, and bacon wrapped in a twelve-inch tortilla. Hash browns and coffee on the side.

Losing weight is part of the experience of the big bike ride, but so is this burrito.

I remember the first day of this trip, staying at the home of Bill Testerman, my first Warm Showers host. Over dinner, Bill told me that cyclists who do the Northern Tier lose their appetite in the beginning; then a switch flips in your system, and you can't stop consuming calories. I remember meeting the three cycling college graduates at the bicycle-only campsite between Mazama and Winthrop, how they were going through a big jar of peanut butter every day. I've been trying to eat peanut butter and jelly on English muffins every morning since then—such an affordable source of protein. But now, 26 days into this trip, I'm done with peanut butter. Bring on the big wrap of bacon and eggs.

Tonight I'm staying at The Bicycle Bunkhouse in Dalbo. Don and Sherry converted one of their barns into a bicycle tourer's oasis: flat screen TV, free food in the fridge, rooms with mattresses, couches. You could sleep up to 30 cyclists if you wanted to. I shouldn't be surprised that places like this exist, but I am. It's just good to know these places exist because folks like Don and Sherry exist.

Don came by to introduce himself and offered some advice on routes. I needed it, because I'm going off the ACA-mapped route system tomorrow and will head toward La Crosse to meet Sue. Don pointed out some bike paths I can take that go in the direction I'm heading.

I will miss using the ACA maps. I'm grateful for the information they provided. Not having to worry about where to eat and camp frees the mind to find other things to think about, or not think about.

Lately I've been thinking about Joseph Conrad. When I can't sleep in the tent, I reread *Heart of Darkness*. In preparation for the trip, I downloaded a PDF version of the novella. I haven't read it in a couple of years, and I think this is the fourth or fifth time I've gone through it cover to cover. I enjoy rereading books because they stay the same while I, the reader, change, making the reading experience different each time. I think this works only for books that have depth, though: literature, if you will.

I tell my students that I define "literature" as "crafted writing that speaks to the human condition." The definition always spawns a good debate as to whether or not this is a good working definition. We bat around various ways of approaching the concept of literature; the Wikipedia definition always seems to make its way into the discussion.

But this is just a setup for the real discussion I want to have, one that focuses on levels of interpreting text. I see four levels of interpretation:

1. Surface interpretation: there is no need to interpret, because the writing is not designed for interpretation (for example, a Harlequin romance novel).

2. Intellectual interpretation: this is what we like to do in university literature courses, deconstruct text and find hidden meaning, so as to explain character development, plot summary, and so on.

3. Emotional interpretation: this can happen in a university classroom, but it doesn't happen often. It's when the reader has an honest emotional response to the work of literature. When this happens, it often interferes with the reader's ability to interpret the work intellectually.

4. Metaphysical interpretation: a work of literature that affects you so much that it alters the way you are.

I tell my students that we are constantly engaged in surface-level interpretation. If a work does not require interpretation, then it is not literature. If "literature" is text that informs us of the human condition, then it needs to be deep enough to require interpretation, simply because this is endemic of the human condition.

Most of my students are skilled at intellectual interpretation, especially those who took Advanced Placement English courses in high school. They know what patterns to look for. Intellectual interpretation takes on the lion's share of the course, since the course objectives target this type of reading.

You have to be careful with emotional interpretations in the classroom. It's important to honor them, but the students who are doing intellectual interpretation don't want to venture into the affective—it's not comfortable. If I see a student having an emotional response to the text, we usually take the discussion offline and meet during office hours. That way, the student gets to express the interpretation with the time and space required to make sense of his emotions.

The metaphysical interpretation doesn't happen often in my classrooms. I can count on one hand the number of times a student was so affected by the literature that they had to stop the class, just so they could fully confront their reading. The times this has taken place, I've actually removed the students from the course and provided them with individual curricula different from the course syllabus, so they could take the time to delve into that specific work. It's important to honor a metaphysical interpretation. It doesn't happen often, so when it does, you have to encourage it.

I liken the levels of interpretation to swimming under water:

1. A surface interpretation is like swimming on the surface—no need to go underwater to see what's down there.

2. An intellectual interpretation is like holding your breath and swimming underwater for a while, but you remain close to the surface, and sunlight enables you to see through the water.

3. An emotional interpretation requires the swimmer, or reader, to swim deeper and stay under longer. You learn how to hold your breath. You get used to the darkness of the depth. Most importantly, you know how to come back up from the depths so as not to get the literary bends.

4. A metaphysical interpretation requires the reader to stay underwater for an unnatural period of time. You develop literary gills—you breathe the water. Water consumes you. So when you eventually surface, you aren't quite sure what is surface and what are the depths.

In spite of all the literature I've been exposed to, I can think of only a dozen books that have altered the way I am. If I were to give "Dave's Top Ten" works of literature that changed me forever, the list would read like this:

1. *Collected Poems* (Weslyan Poetry Series), by James Wright

2. *Catching Fire*, by Jack Gilbert

3. *Heart of Darkness*, by Joseph Conrad

4. *Zen and the Art of Motorcycle Maintenance: An Inquiry Into Values*, by Robert Pirsig

5. *An Inquiry into the Good*, by Nishida Kitaro

6. *Laughing Lost in the Mountains: Poems of Wang Wei*, by Wang Wei

7. *American Primitive*, by Mary Oliver

8. *A River Runs Through It and Other Stories*, by Norman Maclean

9. *Slaughterhouse-Five*, by Kurt Vonnegut

10. *Cowboys Are My Weakness*, by Pam Houston

It's good to know the books that have changed who you are. It's good to go back and reread them and remember the impact they had on you, and how you've grown since reading them last. That said, I'm also reminded of an ancient Chinese proverb: *It is better to travel ten thousand miles than read ten thousand books.*

DAY TWENTY-EIGHT

Five in the morning. There's no need to hurry. Thanks to the Bicycle Bunkhouse, I slept on a mattress last night, so most of my gear is still packed in the panniers, which are still on the bike. This morning's exit will be simple, except for the coffee made in a coffee maker and bread toasted in a toaster. Appliances seem like a luxury. But maybe staying at the Bicycle Bunkhouse, having a blend of cycling and domestic conveniences, is good transitioning to life after the ride.

Tonight I'll stay in a state park, then on Sunday in a hotel, then another state park. Then Sue and I will stay in a bed and breakfast, then another bed and breakfast, then a friend's house, then we'll cap it off with a four-star hotel before riding home. Credit card camping. I won't be complaining, but it will be different than the tent and sleeping bag.

In my early twenties, backpacking through Europe and Southeast Asia, I learned quickly that the less money you spend, the more interesting the journey is. Not that I had a choice back then; I could only afford to spend ten dollars a day. But that forced the adventures: sleeping on trains, in schoolyards, in the homes of people we met along the way, hitchhiking, trekking, eating whatever was available. I remember the details of those trips vividly, in large part because I learned how good it can be to live with just what you need, what you can carry on your back.

For the past month I've lived off what I can carry on the bike.

And other than eating periodically in restaurants, there hasn't been much overhead for this trip, and that's helped make it an amazing experience. When I used to motorcycle camp with friends in eastern Oregon we would camp out occasionally, but more often we'd stay in hotels and eat in restaurants. It was easy and convenient, and we could afford to do it. We all rode BMW motorcycles and had well-paying jobs. This trip is interesting because, although I could have afforded hotels and a constant intake of restaurant food, hotels create a comfortable buffer. Sometimes, like on my birthday, after having ridden 125 miles through Montana, the comfort buffer was appreciated. But I'm glad most of this trip has been spent in the tent. And I'm grateful for people like Don and Sherry who invented the Bicycle Bunkhouse, and the hosts for my Warm Shower stays, and the Honey Hub—all these places I've stayed with people who made the choice to bring in not only me but anyone cycling across the country. It's quite a network and quite a community; I'm glad I've become part of it.

It will be interesting to see what the next bicycling journey will be. I hope it will involve Sue, the two of us rolling down the road on touring bikes, mapping our way from place to place. But I don't know if that will be the case. Ending this trip with Sue at bed-and-breakfasts will be great. That's what we like to do together, and it would only make sense that it's how we would bike for four days together. But it's not how I've spent my time biking on my own. Will Sue and I, as a couple, learn how to bike as I've been biking this last month? We'll have to wait and find out how much interest this has for her.

I may simply continue to make these rides on my own. Maybe this is what happens when your kids grow up and leave the house: you learn new ways to enjoy the company of your life partner, but you also learn new ways to enjoy your own company.

I'm happy to finish this journey with Sue and not alone. The less money you spend, the more adventure you have; but I don't want money, or the lack of it, to prevent me from embracing what is most important. What is most important to me is Sue. I could have spent less money, could have stealth-camped like the twin brothers were doing back in Washington State, just sleeping on the side of the road at the end of the day. I could have eaten more from grocery stores instead of enjoying the occasional breakfast burrito or pancake breakfast. But that's not what my trip has been. Money can be a nemesis on a trip like this, if you're bent on spending as much or as little as possible. I'm glad that funds have been a moot issue, something I didn't give much thought to. Camping over hotels was more of an aesthetic choice than a financial one. Staying in people's homes along the way was an opportunity to receive generosity.

I keep thinking back to Father Odo at the abbey. Because he's a Benedictine monk, he could not refuse me: as a member of his order, he had to take me in. But he made the choice, when he was twenty years old, to be a monk. That was his choice more than fifty years ago, and that choice makes his generosity possible.

I want Sue to share in this type of experience. What cynicism I had regarding the human condition has dissipated. I am full of stories that illustrate the generosity of those I've encountered on this journey. It's only natural that I would want Sue to meet these people. Whether she embraces this type of experience is up to her; all I can do is tell her how amazing it is. I'm sure we'll find some middle ground, some way to share a long ride. Because compromising does not mean not getting what you want, so much as recognizing what the other person wants and blending that in. At least that's how it's played out for Sue and me.

I wanted this trip, and it was designed for a specific type of experience. In a few days Sue and I will experience a different kind of trip. I will enjoy the good company of my beautiful wife as we sleep in comfy beds and eat fattening meals. And I'll have to keep a sense of perspective: one type of bike touring is not necessarily better than the other. They are different and have different intents: one for the generation of solitude and the other for the reconnection of a relationship. I am fortunate, and grateful, to have both.

It's noon, and I'm in a sports bar in Wyoming, Minnesota, having a couple of beers and a salad. Probably not the smartest choice, beers in the middle of a hot 80-mile bike ride, but I'm treating myself. Today is mostly bike path, I'm a day closer to the end of the trip, and even though I'm trying not to think about the ending, I can't help myself. It's just happening.

It's in part sparked by meeting Jake at the Bicycle Bunkhouse. He started his bicycling trip in Portland and is ending it today in Minneapolis. He'll visit family before shipping his bike, and himself, back to the west coast. Because last night was his last night, he was in a reflective mood. We spoke about what his journey was like and what he learned along the way. We'd stayed in many of the same places and met many of the same people; our mutual trips had a surprising amount of overlap. But he's 28 years old, single, and had never ridden a bicycle more than 50 miles at a time before his trip from Oregon to Minnesota; his perspective was wildly different than mine. I asked what he had learned from the last month and, after some time, he said he wants to:

- continually comprehend that gestures, both big and small, can make or break a person's spirit.

- be unafraid to have his voice heard rather than shying away.

- be more self-confident. This journey isn't something most people would accomplish. Doing so gave him a tangible reason to be more confident. He knows he biked up Lolo Pass—he can always remember that accomplishment in times of personal doubt.

- worry less.

- avoid getting lost in technology, the phone, or the Internet.

- be more respectful toward women.

That's a pretty good list. He kept a journal during the ride, tracking these ideas as he rolled down the road.

We talked about how the journey provides the opportunity for reflection, especially at the end. The trick, I said, is to figure out how to ritualize these opportunities for reflection in our daily domestic lives. Jake disagreed: he said the trick is always to go on journeys.

Sometimes, I cannot learn. Why did I have two beers with lunch? Now I'm sitting in the shade at the side of the bike path, ready to take a big fat nap. Which actually feels great: watching other cyclists go by, listening to the breeze. It's a nice change of pace. Today is an 80-mile day, and I have hours to go before I need to arrive at Afton State Park. There's no hurry. In this moment I'm embracing the slow, aided by the mental lubrication of hops and barley.

I'm reflecting on Jake's reflections, his list of things learned on his journey. So far, I can think of three things that stand out in terms of what I've learned:

1. Solitude feeds the marriage, and marriage feeds the solitude. At the beginning of the trip, I thought it was binary: I loved Sue or I loved solitude, although I had a sense that the two complemented each other. Now I know they do. To be a good husband, I first have to be a good me, and I love to be alone. So, be alone, and then go home and be good to Sue.

2. The Northern Tier Diet worked—I've lost weight. But this is not the first time I've shed pounds; I did it almost every time I raced Ironman. I'd train, drop weight, race, and put it back on. This time I have no intention of putting it back on, so I called Sue and asked her to recommend a nutritionist. She emailed me the contact information of someone she's worked with out of Madison. I promptly emailed the nutritionist, explaining my situation and requesting an appointment. This time will be different. I won't try to do it alone, and I will try to do it.

3. I need to exercise my humanity more consistently. What I'd like to see from myself is a real-time willingness to exercise generosity with the resources I have. To share more. To be as giving as the people I've met on this trip. If I don't learn that now, then a good portion of this trip will have been wasted.

It was a tough bike ride to the campground. The weather forecast was off by about fifteen degrees; the afternoon hit temperatures up to 95. But heat is just part of the deal in early August. Mosquitos are Minnesota's state bird.

Once I arrived at Afton State Park, I went for a refreshing swim in the St. Croix River, then quickly sprayed my body with mosquito repellent and rode my bike back up to the top of the hill, where the golf course adjacent to the park has a clubhouse. A turkey club sandwich and a couple of beers later, all was good again.

The legs were complaining a bit biking back to the campsite. Four days and four hundred miles on a fully loaded touring bike—no wonder they aren't happy. I've promised them that tomorrow is nothing more than fifty miles and, at the end, a hotel room with a bed. I should spend tomorrow afternoon laying back, letting the legs rest up for one more 70-mile push into La Crosse. And those miles will run along the Mississippi River, nice and flat.

WISCONSIN

DAY TWENTY-NINE

The journey must be nearing completion, because I didn't get out of the tent this morning until well past seven. I woke when I normally do, around 4:30, but soon started dozing in and out of sleep. Periodically, I could hear a deer near the tent eating grass. But then I'd go back to sleep, and wake, and wonder if it was a deer or a dream of a deer.

Sue woke me with a phone call. She suggested I get up and make coffee so I'd be a better conversationalist, which I did. But I took my time. I've done a good job at "slow" on the bike on this trip, but that hasn't transferred into the campsite. In the morning, I typically get things packed up and on the bike so I can ride. Today is a 50-miler, which is only five hours in the saddle. I don't have to hurry. In fact, I'm staying at a hotel tonight, so arriving early would just involve waiting for check-in.

I'm doing what most bicycle tourers do: sleep in a bit, heat up some coffee, have a warm breakfast, look around, and eventually put the stuff back on the bike and ride. This system works for those who are crossing the entire country, from Seattle to Maine. My trip is ending about three fifths of the way across. I don't think I could sustain a pace of 80-100 miles a day all the way to Maine. I can already feel the burnout.

I've met people like that, who go coast to coast, then north or south for a while before going coast to coast again. Those are the retired, the independently wealthy, or those who have figured out how to do this so cheaply that they can do it indefinitely. I've read of people who crowd-source their journeys: donate to my cause, so I can have the adventure you can't.

I also took the time to hit the restroom for a shave and tooth-brushing. The men's room was a wreck: the light didn't work, the aroma was far too fragrant, there were discarded garments left in the corner. Because I'm the only bicycle camper in the park, I decided to check out the women's room. What a different story: functional lighting, clean, and a container full of hand sanitizer.

I should get the bike packed up, but I just keep sitting in this campsite, watching the St. Croix River run by. The next time I plan a tour, I should allow enough time to do 50-mile days. I should have learned how to do this back in Washington.

At this point, you would think I would have learned the lesson of how to take my time. I just did a proper bike cleaning of all the working parts: the rear cassette, front cassette, chain, brake cables, brake calipers, brake discs. There was a great deal of dirt and grime on them all. For about a week I've put up with a squeaky bike, thinking I'd give it a good cleaning when I got back to the house and garage. That's how things go wrong on a trip like this: you see the end, and you think you can wait until then to solve the problem. In this case, the only problem is the irritating noises coming from the bike's components. It took me all of twenty minutes to flip the bike over, get out the cleaning solution and brushes, and clean up the bike. Not only will this minimize the risk of bike failure, but it will make for a better riding experience.

Yesterday, I wrote about lessons learned on this journey. This lesson regarding time, to do one thing at a time and do it well, is a big one, too big to solve on a one-month bike ride. I've been fighting this problem ever since graduate school. Before grad school, before I had numerous jobs, courses, and research essays, time was plentiful. I was also lucky enough to have financial support when I was an undergrad, so there was no need to work then. As an English major I spent my days reading books, going to class, and talking about the books I read. Lots of time.

I never properly learned how to manage time. I've gone through phases of life when I gave up on the concept completely. Five years ago I went through a *Yes Man* phase. When the movie starring Jim Carrey came out, I was intrigued by the notion that life could be better if you just said "yes" to every opportunity that came your way. I defined "luck" as "when preparation meets opportunity," and I wondered if the preparation was necessary, if embracing every opportunity would give you the experience necessary to be prepared for whatever came your way.

It was a good learning experience. I ended up working with countless nonprofit organizations in the greater Milwaukee community, became the "go to" guy on campus because I could "get things done," continued to train for Ironman triathlons, engaged in every activity my kids were involved in, traveled to Kenya and northern India with students to enact service projects. I said yes to it all. And all that stimulation was a bit addictive. All the praise I received from people telling me I was a go-getter. Our culture rewards those who work hard, and I was amply rewarded.

Getting out of that mindset was difficult. In fact, I hope this bike ride is one of the final stages in the transformation back to my authentic, reflective, introverted self. I gave up a great deal to become the Yes Man. It wasn't who I am; it was an affect I put on in the hope that I could become that person.

That's the beauty of burnout. Burnout forces you to stop everything you're doing, which is what happened a year ago. I was done. After rising to the level of Dean of Students, after double- and triple-booking myself for meetings day in and day out, I ran into a professor in the hallway. It was late June, and he was on summer break, something I gave up when I decided to be Dean of Students and work on a twelve-month contract. The professor, who is a friend of mine, was telling me about all the time he was spending with his kids at their summer house up north. How he was riding his bike daily but not training for any particular event. He sounded happy, and when I walked away from that conversation, I realized that he had something I had given up: the time it takes to be happy.

Which goes back to Nishida. Happiness involves some suffering, some surrender. Happiness is, for me at least, slowness. Going slow up the mountain pass, going slow into a headwind, or just pedaling down a Minnesota bike path, going slow for no reason other than that you're happy. Right now, I've learned this lesson. Let's hope it sticks: that I continue to say "yes" to opportunity, but one opportunity at a time.

Here are two rules I will follow on the next bike tour:

1. Don't get on the bike until you are ready to get on the bike.

2. Don't get on the bike until the bike is ready for you to get on the bike.

The bike is clean, and so am I. Feeling good as we roll out of the campground. Wisconsin is seven miles away. Time to cross the Mississippi.

Sitting again on the side of the road, but this time on a manicured lawn. Or an extension of someone's lawn, since it's the side of the road. I'm definitely not in eastern Montana.

Now that I'm back in the saddle, I'm realizing that if you bike 50 to 60 miles a day, you maximize your time out of the saddle. If you bike 80 to 100 miles a day, you maximize time in the saddle. And for me it's more about being on the bike, since the bicycle is a vehicle for non-thought. The more hours of sustained biking you get, the deeper you venture into non-thought, or into thought. Either way.

I could work at enacting non-thought off the bike. But to be honest, it just seems easier on it.

~

Today is going to be interesting, since I've already decided where I'll be spending the night. I'm already ten miles down the road. That means I get only another 40 today. We'll see how I feel about that when I arrive in Stockholm.

What I learned may seem painfully obvious, but it's rarely obvious to me: it doesn't have to be all one way or all another. You don't always have to bike 50 or 100 miles. You can mix it up. The beauty of the ACA maps is that they give you countless options regarding where you're going to camp for the night, so it's quite easy, at the beginning of a given day, to decide how far you're going to go and what type of experience you hope to have.

For me, the bicycle tour is an activity that lends itself to Nishida's sense of *pure experience*. I do lose my sense of self when I'm on Salsa, riding down a straight road for hours on end. Maybe 100-mile days are just an extended engagement with this sense of moving meditation. It certainly makes me feel alive, and that feeling makes me want to keep on pedaling.

It makes me wonder how many miles Sue and I would do if we did a tour together. On our morning phone call, we were laughing at how I carried all these cooking spices with me across the country but rarely used them. If I were touring and camping with her, we'd be using them. She's a master of culinary skills, whether in the kitchen or the campground. It would make for a fun addition to the overall experience. Maybe she can teach me a thing or two about bike touring.

This evening was an exercise in not-thought. I checked into the Spring Street Inn in Stockholm, Wisconsin. My online research didn't show any camping between where I was last night and where I'll be tomorrow, so I opted for a nice room that had an affordable rate in a town that has more art galleries than other shops combined.

One of the other shops was a pie shop, though, so once settled in, I took a shower, did some laundry, and went and bought a pie—and a sandwich and some beer. Back to the inn I went with my bounty and watched two mindless movies, *Expendables 3 and Madagascar Penguins*. That's about as much not-thought as I can handle for one night.

I reflect on the balance between thought and non-thought. It's been the driving force of this journey. Tonight's experience of not-thought was a welcome change of pace. It's also another re-entry into normal life. After tonight, I'll set up my tent for the last time. After that, I'll be sleeping in a bed with my beautiful wife. It sounds good. I'll miss the tent and living off the bike, but I'm doing my best to prepare for the transition back to suburban reality, and right now that means sleeping in a cozy inn, eating pie and drinking beer.

This trip has been a lot of work. Beyond riding a bike 2,500 miles, the thought I experienced during the trip was demanding. I tell my students that thinking is hard work, as it should be. You're processing knowledge in meaningful ways, receiving new data, making it fit with the existing information in your long-term memory. The emphasis on melding thought with non-thought has been both beneficial and enjoyable. It's turned out to be the purpose of the ride.

There is a relationship between solitude and marriage. They balance each other, the way non-thought balances thought, one feeding the other.

DAY THIRTY

Seven-thirty in the morning. I'm having coffee, eggs, and bacon in a diner in Nelson. Today is the last day carrying all the gear. Tomorrow is a rest day, and the day after that Evan drops off Sue so we can bike back together, and when that happens I'll leave most of the gear for Evan to drive back home. I decided to start early and enjoy the bike with all its weight one more time. Those first ten miles are always physiologically interesting; getting the legs up to speed works in concert with getting the Salsa up to speed.

It's surprising that there have been no major physical side effects on this big bike ride. You push your body this hard, and you would think something would snap. Maybe it's the result of rolling slow, pacing the body instead of pushing it. That ties into the relationship between mind and body: slow thought, slow roll. I've thoroughly enjoyed the thought process this big bike ride presented, the countless hours in the saddle working ideas from one point to the other, the continuity between miles and ideas. The more I do this, especially these high-mileage days, the happier I am.

The quality and quantity of the cycling seem to be in sync with the quality and quantity of the happiness that ensues, especially on these high-mileage days.

Last fall, at the Lilly North Conference, I met Jeannie Loeb. She teaches too and gives thought to how to get her students to think well. She spoke to this idea of how the brain works best when it's happily doing what it's designed to do:

When we are in a positive state, the brain is actually functioning physically in ways that support learning. We are more creative, better able to solve problems, and more likely to retain information. Establishing and promoting a strong rapport with our students puts us all in a positive state of mind which then contributes to cognitive functioning. Positivity can take many forms – joy, gratitude, interest, pride, inspiration, amusement, etc. It is beneficial to be constantly thinking of ways we can promote happiness and positivity.

How can a cyclist experience a morning like this and not be happy? Before eating a protein-heavy breakfast, I watched the sunrise over the Mississippi River. Happiness, even in this cycling environment, is not a foregone conclusion. Happiness is a choice. My brain likes it when I choose to be happy, and my body likes biking down Highway 35 early on a Monday morning. This moment of happiness is no accident.

A full month on the road and only a few moments of melancholy. How do I transfer this into my domestic life back in Milwaukee? That's a problem worth pondering.

It has to do with having one big challenge. Not more than one: just one. This big bike ride is a great challenge. It stretches me in any number of ways. Not only has it provided new experiences and ideas, it also solidifies the ideas I have about marriage, family, and career.

One big challenge, and go at it slow. Let yourself think about it, and let yourself non-think about it. Let the challenge take you to the top of the mountain pass, and then enjoy the descent.

Time to get back on the bike.

Bibliography

Abe Masao. *Zen and Western Thought*. Ed. William R. LaFleur. Honolulu: University of Hawaii Press, 1985.

Csikszentmihalyi, Mihaly. *Creativity: Flow and the Psychology of Discovery and Invention*. New York: HarperCollins, 2009.

De Botton, Alain. *The Art of Travel*. New York: Vintage International, 2004.

Doyle, Terry. *The New Science of Learning: How to Learn in Harmony with your Brain*. Sterling, VA: Stylus Publishing, 2013.

Duggan, William. *Strategic Intuition: The Creative Spark in Human Achievement*. New York: Columbia University Press, 2007.

Howell, David. *In Sixteen Hands of Shadow*. Whitefish Bay: Red Roan Press, 2004.

Kundera, Milan. *Slowness: A Novel*. New York: Harper Perennial, 1997.

Loeb, Jeannie. *Lilly Conference Keynote Reflection: Grey Matters when Teaching*. June 20, 2014.

Nishida, Kitaro. *An Inquiry into the Good*. Trans. Nasao Abe and Christopher Ives. New Haven: Yale, 1990.

---. "An Explanation of Beauty." *Monumenta Nipponica: Studies in Japanese Culture*. vol. 42, 2, summer 1987.

Peck, M. Scott. *The Road Less Traveled, Timeless Edition: A New Psychology of Love, Traditional Values and Spiritual Growth*. New York: Touchstone, 2003.

Pirsig, Robert. *Zen and the Art of Motorcycle Maintenance*. New York: William Morrow, 1974.

Stafford, William. *Stories that could be true: New and collected poems*. New York: 1977.

Storre, Anthony. *Solitude: A Return to the Self.* New York: Free Press, 2005.

Tadashi Ogawa. "The Kyoto School of Philosophy and Phenomenology." *Japanese Phenomenology: Phenomenology as the Trans-cultural Philosophical Approach.* Ed. Yoshihiro Nitta and Hirotaka Tatematsu. Boston: D. Reidel, 1979.

Wilson, Eric G. *Against Happiness: In Praise of Melancholy.* New York: Sarah Crichton Books, 2009.